American Automobile Album

EARLY DAYS

THE

MODEL T

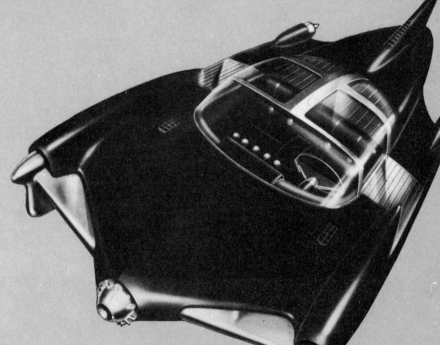

TOMORROW

AMERICAN AUTOMOBILE ALBUM

WILLIAM H. McGAUGHEY

OVER 250 PHOTOGRAPHS

E. P. Dutton & Co., Inc.

PUBLISHER

NEW YORK · 1954

TO

BILL, ANDY

DAVE AND MARGARET

ROBUST AMERICANS

WHOSE FOCUSES ARE ON THE FUTURE

Contents

AMERICAN AUTOMOBILE ALBUM

ONLY THE BRAVE

Road conditions discouraged all but the intrepid driver. Rarely did a woman get behind the wheel of a gasoline car, and scarcely ever did she venture forth alone. It proved a photographer's prize, therefore, to catch mother and daughter, above, coaxing a 1903 air-cooled Franklin across a stream.

Chapter 1

EARLY DAYS

THE ADVENTUROUS FEW

AMERICA was restless. Klondike fever sent thousands scurrying northward. Railroads lured multitudes west. Cities beckoned the farmer's children. Americans by the million itched to go somewhere, *anywhere.*

For a while, the bicycle helped satisfy the urge for independent travel. The sport had its limitations, but by 1900 ten million Americans had taken to the two-wheelers. It helped focus attention on America's muddy, dusty, rutted roads, which in dirty weather kept millions of families largely immobile.

Over these roads one day chuffed a four-wheel contraption, emitting a series of machine-gun like explosions and a cloud of disagreeable fumes. Skeptics were legion, and their jibes and jeers reached crescendo proportions. But an adventurous few spotted the automobile—even before it acquired a generic name—as a fascinating new gadget that promised real sport. These mud-mired adventurers were out for fun, but they succeeded in fostering a revolution greater than Genghis Khan's.

In 1900, some 76,000,000 people lived in the United States. A vast majority lived on farms, where 18,000,000 horses and mules aided their efforts. As for automobiles, over the broad landscape that is America, less than 4,000 could be found.

INTREPID TRAVELERS

Motoring beckoned only the brave. Road maps were nonexistent. On venturing beyond the city limits, the automobilist tried to follow a railroad or telegraph line to the next town. Rural roads often proved his nemesis. If he escaped the mud, some vexatious mechanical difficulty usually managed to engulf him. If he miraculously avoided either, then he still had to tussle with another thorn—a hostile social attitude directed at him and his noisy vehicle. Horses bolted at his approach. Bicyclists fumed. Anxious mothers, on hearing the motorist head down Main Street, snatched their young from the curbstone. In New York, Central Park authorities considered banning cars, in Jersey voters boycotted politicians who drove them, in Illinois an irate citizenry fostered a Farmers' Anti-Automobile League.

But groups of intrepid men, and a few women, persisted in driving. Despite bad roads, unsafe bridges, uncertain mechanisms, these adventurous Americans coaxed their cars into countless villages and hamlets that rarely attracted outsiders. The begoggled intruders created a new restlessness in smug, insular America.

BARN LOFT PROSPECTORS

With gold fever sweeping America near the end of the century, hundreds of thousands sought fortunes in Alaska and the Yukon. But other Americans stayed home getting their excitement in trying to produce a spark in crude gasoline engines. These stay-at-homes started a flow of gold, in product wealth and wages, that eventually made the Klondike bonanza seem like small change in the till.

At first, though, it was a discouraging business for the automobile pioneers. Neighbors expressed concern over the ominous noises coming from their lofts and woodsheds. Bankers and investors avoided them like the plague. From a safe distance, the town sages decried their fiddling and made frequent pronouncements that "there's no future in the horseless carriage."

For many, there was not. For Duryea, Haynes, Olds, King, Winton, Maxwell, Ford and others, there was fame. For some, there was fortune. For a few, fabulous wealth.

HOOSIER PIONEER
Elwood Haynes, a Hoosier schoolmaster who found the natural gas boom profitable, provided the idea and funds for one of America's first successful automobiles. Built in the Apperson brothers' machine shop, the car had its first public trial on July 4, 1894 on Kokomo's Pumpkin Vine Pike. Haynes' love of design, plus his metallurgical skill, was destined to shift the trend away from "horseless carriages" and provide the automobile with a form of its own.
Brown Bros.

12

Doctors needed better transportation, and this resourceful physician, Dr. Hiram H. Bardwell, built an electric car himself in 1901. It was the first automobile ever built in Flint, Michigan.
Crooks Studio

The American automobile grew out of a need for adequate personal transportation. Charles and Frank Duryea, credited by some authorities with making the first American gasoline car in Springfield, Massachusetts, in 1893, had been in the bicycle business. Elwood Haynes, a one-time Hoosier schoolmaster, discouraged because Indiana's quagmires hindered travel by buggy, commissioned the Apperson brothers to build him a one-horsepower vehicle. Young inventor Hiram Percy Maxim, fed-up with pedaling by bicycle nightly over back roads to court a young Salem, Massachusetts, lady, managed to propel a $30 Columbia tandem tricycle with a homemade gasoline engine.

Such ingenious tinkerers managed to start commercial enterprises for building and merchandising automobiles. But countless other inventive efforts resulted only in working models of motor vehicles which never gained acceptance. Over a half century, more than 1,500 different makes of automobiles have grown out of the minds and hands of American inventors.

Dissatisfied when Alexander Winton refused to service a car he'd bought from the Winton Company, James Ward Packard decided to build an automobile himself. Here is his 1901 model, with four cautious Warren, Ohio girls in the tonneau.

Packard Motor Co.

Brown Bros.

FLORAL FANFARE

Famed society playboy and wit, Harry Lehr, is shown above with the first Mrs. John Jacob Astor at Newport in 1901. Floral decorations for automobiles were the vogue at the colony's gala lawn fêtes. Dowagers also staged racing contests around obstacle courses set up on their lawns.

Newport races soon outgrew the lawns of society matrons, and took to a specially built track. Here mechanics are getting cars ready for a racing meet for wealthy sportsmen. Chain-driven car above is a French-made Panhard, a favorite with occupants of Newport and Lenox villas.

A.M.A.
(Automobile Mfgs. Ass'n)

The square canopy top, fringe all around, distinguished the 1901 Waverly Electric.

Albert Mecham

HIGH SOCIETY HOBBY

In its early years, the automobile occupied a gold-plated pedestal. The public viewed it as a rich man's toy. Its usage made society page headlines. Automobile ownership customarily marked a man of distinction, a millionaire sportsman or a high society member.

America's upper crust had, however, little to do with the native product. Their cars were imported from Europe, beginning with Mrs. O. H. P. Belmont's expensive French machine brought to Newport in 1897. The Vanderbilts, the Drexels, the Whitneys followed suit. Within two years it had become a fad for Newport's aristocracy to proceed down Bellevue Avenue and along Ocean Drive by motor car.

Mrs. Belmont, who delighted in startling innovations, introduced a new wrinkle to an expensive sport. One September afternoon she turned her lawn into an obstacle course, marked with golf flags, for an automobile race. *The New York Times'* reporter recorded that Colonel Jack Astor, at the tiller of an electric, "steered with the same cool-headed dash that distinguished him while serving under fire at Santiago."

To climax the summer season, members of the 400 set paraded in flower-decorated automobiles around the Belmont estate. Mr. Belmont, with Mrs. Stuyvesant Fish at his side, led one procession in a runabout decorated with yellow field flowers. Next came Mr. J. W. Gerard with Mrs. Belmont, and behind them Mr. Harry Lehr, the wit, with Mrs. John Jacob Astor. Their vehicles abounded with blue hydrangeas, daisies, and other flowers. After an evening of dining and dancing, the procession turned homeward at midnight. "Every vehicle," a chronicler noted, "was brilliantly illuminated with countless little glow lights interspersed among the floral wreaths" and the procession of scintillating vehicles glided over the dark country roads leading into Newport "like a veritable pageant of fairy chariots."

Most celebrated after-dinner speaker of his era, Chauncey Depew, is shown in a 1903 steam car. Depew, right, served as a judge of the Cosmopolitan Race, one of the first auto races in America. It was run between New York and Irvington-on-the-Hudson.
Underwood & Underwood

THE FAST SET

Some heavy-powered, fast-stepping models came out of European workshops, which were far ahead of America in developing cars. Horsepower generated by American cars was puny by comparison. So wealthy young bloods here imported the big, swift European makes and proceeded to stir up clouds of dust along the Eastern seaboard.

One well-known sportsman, William K. Vanderbilt, ventured from Newport to New York in his Daimler in the fall of 1900. Attired in leather jacket, large goggles and patent leather cap, Vanderbilt was accompanied by his French chauffeur and footman, similarly garbed. His wife took the train down from Newport and waited all day at the Waldorf-Astoria for him.

Somewhat weather-beaten, Vanderbilt arrived at the hotel late at night, reporting that rain and unfamiliarity with the roads had delayed him. His fastest time had been 40 m.p.h., but he'd traveled only short distances at that speed. Vanderbilt's time began to look good, however, when J. Dunbar Wright, second vice president of the Automobile Club, made the Newport to New York trip a few weeks later. Wright, driving a Winton, required four days for the journey. The drive from Newport, it appeared, was more of a hardship than a sport.

Vanderbilt's exploits continued to keep him in the news. They also advanced his reputation for sportsmanship and courteous behavior. In 1900, driving between Garden City and Jamaica, he challenged a Long Island train to a race, and roared into Jamaica a good three minutes ahead. In Manhattan on another occasion, he had an unexpected encounter with a fish wagon at 51st Street and Fifth Avenue. Vanderbilt slammed on the

MAN OF DISTINCTION
The high jinks of rich men's sons usually provoked social censure, but William K. Vanderbilt, Jr., managed to retain public approval, despite a craving for high-speed motoring. A leading sportsman of his day, he both participated in and fostered road races, overland tours and other events which tested the mechanical proficiency of cars and the skill of drivers. Shown above, he awaits his turn in a hill-climbing contest.
A.M.A

brakes, but the car crashed into the wagon, spilling fish out on the street. The millionaire approached the fish peddler, gave his name and insisted that the injured horse be treated at his own stables.

"It is a fortunate thing that the great majority of automobilists are gentlemen, and, when any accident occurs, they do all in their power to remedy matters," a leading motor publication commented.

Not so generous about motors and motorists, however, were other influential voices of the time. Sensing a popular issue, *The New York World* denounced the automobile as "an expensive luxury for the man who does not need one. It is well named the 'devil wagon.'"

America's rising middle class, however, was beginning to covet ownership of this promising badge of social prestige, the automobile.

Here is a group of sportsmen ready for run over a hard surface in 1904 Peugeot. Harry Payne Whitney is standing with back to camera, conferring with a driver.

A.M.A.

State laws often demanded that motorists stop when they saw a horse approaching. If requested, the motorist had to get out and lend assistance.

OUTWARD BOUND

Venturing away from the city was an appealing concept to motorists. Getting home again, though, often presented a problem—sometimes mechanical, sometimes social, sometimes financial.

More than any transportation device, the automobile provided the adventurous city dweller with the means for exploring the countryside, scaling the hilltops, penetrating the recesses of slumbering hamlets and hidden valleys.

But the new means of locomotion had its drawbacks. Roads lacked surfacing, lacked bridges, lacked markings. Horsepower, supplied by farm animals, sometimes was required to supplement the car's mechanical power. Farmers had their views about noisy vehicles that disturbed the Sunday peace, and they had their price for helping vehicle owners get out of trouble.

State laws governing encounters between motorists and animals often were quite strict. Some laws demanded that motorists, on seeing a horse approach, come to a complete stop and lend assistance when needed. Some

18

DOBBIN TO THE RESCUE
Like many other motorists, these travelers who set out bravely in a 1903 Cadillac found it tough to get back. One passenger climbs back into the tonneau entrance after making sure the ropes are fast to the buggy axle.

hostile groups wanted to see the rules of the road more restrictive. In Pennsylvania, the Farmers' Anti-Automobile Association published these rules for drivers:

1. Automobiles traveling on country roads at night must send up a rocket every mile, then wait ten minutes for the road to clear. The driver may then proceed, with caution, blowing his horn and shooting off Roman candles, as before.

2. If the driver of an automobile sees a team of horses approaching, he is to stop, pull over to one side of the road, and cover his machine with a blanket or dust cover which is painted or colored to blend into the scenery, and thus render the machine less noticeable.

3. In case a horse is unwilling to pass an automobile on the road, the driver of the car must take the machine apart as rapidly as possible, and conceal the parts in the bushes.

To counteract hostile attitudes of officialdom, the automobile clubmen resorted to factual presentations and scientific demonstrations. To win over the populace, they agreed on a more dramatic device—an automobile show.

Sunday outings by auto club members, such as this group waiting for Staten Island ferry, focused attention on motoring pleasures. Chief object of curiosity above is a front-wheel-drive Kuhlstein-Vollmer, a German make. Car on the far right is a 1900 Winton, produced by the onetime Cleveland bicycle maker.

DAREDEVIL DESCENDS

To convince the public that automobiles were not as dangerous as they appeared, seventy exhibitors participated in the first Auto Show in 1900 at Madison Square Garden. From the roof garden, cycle champion Joe McDuffie descended a 200-foot artificial hill. By holding a mobile steam car on the incline, he'd show off its brakes to breathless spectators.

SPECTACLE

How to win friends and influence people was a problem uppermost in the deliberations of the Automobile Club of America. An exhibition solely of automobiles was suggested. Albert C. Bostwick, chairman of the committee on runs, tours and expositions, startled conservative members by the audacity of his plans. By the time they caught on to what was happening, the show was ready to open in New York City.

At Madison Square Garden, a circular track one-eighth of a mile long, was laid out. Cluttered with barrels, railing and other impediments to driving, it provoked widespread interest. A 200 foot artificial hill ran up to the roof garden and Joe McDuffie, a celebrated and daring bicycle rider, was persuaded to drive an electric car down it.

The crowds that thronged through the Garden November 3-10, 1900, got their money's worth. Skilled automobile drivers zigzagged around the barrels, darted up inclines, and dodged obstacles strewn in the way of their vehicles. Even to the layman it was evident that these mechanical monsters could be tamed. Families asked for rides around the arena. Interested purchasers sent their coachmen over for morning training sessions in driving. As a climax to the show, on the last night a twelve year old boy drove an electric car around the ring without a mishap. New York was fascinated.

"The automobile has come to stay and in a short time it will displace the horse in many ways," reported *Automobile Topics*.

The automobile was safe for family use, it was demonstrated at the Auto Show. This gentleman driver practices steering in car provided by the International Motor Carriage Co., as mother looks skeptically on.

Brown Bros.

LEGAL SPEED-UP

City fathers proved stone deaf when motorists complained that New York's eight mile-an-hour speed limit was unreasonable. The automobilists resorted, therefore, to a visual demonstration to show that motor cars could be brought to a safe stop at higher speeds.

The Automobile Club of America on May 1, 1902, chalked off Riverside Drive at 109th Street, summoned the press photographers, and conducted a brake test. A 600-pound curved dash Oldsmobile, a four-passenger Apperson, and a half-ton Locomobile steam car glided over the course, were flagged to a halt, and their respective rates of deceleration measured. Over the same measured course galloped a team of horses drawing a Payne Whitney Four-in-Hand. Then came a policeman pedaling a bicycle.

Once the checkers compiled the comparative figures, the Automobile Club officials triumphantly announced the results to the press:

At a speed of 20 miles-an-hour, an automobile could be brought to a complete stop within 60 feet or less; the horse-drawn vehicles required 90 feet. (The policeman got his two-wheeler stopped at 31 feet, two inches.)

Father Knickerbocker surveyed the results and shortly thereafter granted the motorists a legal boost to 20 miles an hour.

PROMPT STOP
To get New York's eight-mile-an-hour speed law lifted, motorists set out to prove scientifically that automobiles could be brought to a halt more quickly than horse-drawn vehicles. Here a 1902 curved-dash Oldsmobile goes through brake test on Riverside Drive at 109th Street, New York.

At hill-climbing contests, spectators munched their lunches and in-haled dust as contestants tried to surmount the steep grades.

ONWARD AND UPWARD

Inexperienced motorists found hills a headache, but the seasoned sports-men regarded them as an irresistible challenge. A successful ascent was a matter of great pride, particularly if the grade was steep enough to enjoy a regional reputation.

Crosscountry motorists stopped overnight at Peekskill, New York, to try to surmount Nelson's Hill, which sports writers termed a "real bête noire." Another popular climb was Eagle Rock Hill in West Orange, New Jersey, known as the "New Jersey Terror." At Wilkes-Barre, Pennsylvania, contest-ants tried to scale "Giants Despair Course," while Dorchester, Massachu-setts, attracted sportsmen to "Dead Horse Hill." Perhaps the most famous event in the East was the "Climb to the Clouds" ascent to Mount Washing-ton which even today puts a strain on motors and nerves.

Hill climbing contests provided excitement for both participants and
spectators. Dust got in the eyes of spectators, and spectators got in the way
of drivers. Upward of 20,000 people were attracted to such events, some
coming by car to park along the route. Well-known figures, such as Thomas
Edison motoring over from Menlo Park, were frequent visitors at the Eagle
Rock climb. The Thanksgiving Day, 1902, event there attracted thirty-two
entries; eighteen started up the hill and thirteen were timed at the finish.
The best effort in the gasoline class was put forth by a 1,050 pound Stevens-
Duryea, which reached the hilltop in three minutes, forty-five seconds, to
establish a new record for the 4,962 feet climb.

A typical news report from Dead Horse Hill related that Willie Houpt
in a Chadwick Six "drove his car at great speed, but when near the top of
the hill was forced to shut off his power to avoid hitting a pedestrian who
had strayed on the course."

But the drivers raced up again, hoping to shatter existing marks.

A few adventurous women took up the sport. The Cuyagoga, (Ohio)
amateur championship was won by Mrs. Kenneth R. Otis, who at a meet
near Cleveland "sent her car flying over the tape and up the long, steep incline; she appeared the very embodiment of speed and daring, bending
over the wheel, with her long veil streaming out behind," according to a
1908 press version.

MR. ASTOR'S HORSE

The start of the New York to Buffalo endurance run in 1901 was
delayed by John Jacob Astor whose yacht *Nourmahal* was late in
docking. Apologizing to officials, he rushed through the crowd
gathered on 58th Street and got his Mercedes car in line for the trek
to Ardsley, the first night's stop. The wealthy sportsman is photo-
graphed at the wheel with a motoring shield protecting his face.

ENDURANCE RUNS

By 8:00 A.M. Monday, September 9, 1901, Plaza Square in New York
was reported as being "thronged by nearly four score of gasoline and steam
vehicles carefully groomed for the fray and simmering gently with stored
energy and endurance." About to begin was the first race of its kind in
America, the New York to Buffalo endurance run.

The start was delayed by the late docking of John Jacob Astor's yacht,
the *Nourmahal*. That wealthy contestant rushed to 58th Street, donned his
motoring shield, and jumped behind the wheel of his Mercedes. His machine was one of forty-nine gasoline vehicles and twenty-six steam cars
entered in the contest.

The run was called off at Rochester on the news of President McKinley's death in Buffalo. In that saddened city, Charles W. Fairbanks, who three years later became vice-president under Theodore Roosevelt, was being interviewed while seated in a product of the Electric Vehicle Co. At right, Auto Club president Albert R. Shattuck, with beard and leggings, chats with the judges at a turn-around point.

The cavalcade made news as it rolled up the Hudson River valley. Some 5,000 spectators cheered as the motorists swept through Yonkers. Ardsley was reached the first night. At Peekskill, the second night's stop, while the drivers were at dinner, a small boy toyed with the lever of a steam car. It promptly moved forward and ran over a twelve-year old girl. Outside Albany, Astor's car mowed down two dogs.

At Rochester, forty-one vehicles still remained in the race. But on getting the news that President McKinley had died in Buffalo, the run was called off.

Endurance runs called for rugged men, reliable machines. On Memorial Day, 1902, sportsmen took a 100-mile jaunt up the Boston Post Road, over the Connecticut line to Southport, then back to the Plaza Hotel in Manhattan.

Some fifty-five American and foreign makes entered the drive. Every car was expected to make the run without a stop except for "tire troubles, police orders, timid horses, closed railroad crossings, blocking of the road, or demands of nature."

The Plaza Hotel also housed the Automobile Club of America, which sponsored many of the early runs. Albert R. Shattuck, its president, curried his beard, pulled on his leggings, and rubbed dusty elbows with other big wheels in the motoring world. He's shown in the adjoining picture.

26

Automobile Old Timers

Country bumpkin and city slicker rubbed elbows at the finish line of a 1901 road race, sponsored by the Automobile Club of America.

Alert to the drawing power of personalities, Shattuck instructed his door man to begin each day by signing three names at the top of the club's guest register: John Jacob Astor, William K. Vanderbilt, Jr., and Harry Payne Whitney. Some days, one or more of the registered men actually could be found inside the club.

John Jacob Astor converted his stable at Rhinecliff, New York, to a garage to house his automobiles. He displayed a preference for foreign makes, as did most wealthy motorists of the day. In the lower picture the second car from the left is a Mors, a French-made gasoline car; the fourth car is a Fiat, an Italian make, also powered by a gasoline motor; the car on the far right is an American-made steam car, the Toledo. All are vintage of 1903-04.

John Jacob Astor's well-equipped stable, converted to a garage, at Rhinecliff, New York.
A.M.A.

27

TOWPATH TO FAME

One November night in 1901, a grease smeared driver sneaked into the employees' entrance of the old Waldorf-Astoria Hotel, having completed an 860 mile trip from Detroit. At the 34th Street service entrance he'd parked his mud coated runabout, an 800 pound, one-cylinder, curved dash Oldsmobile. Priced at $650, the car had scant acceptance from a public accustomed to associating reliability with high prices. To win public confidence, Roy D. Chapin, a twenty-one year old test driver, set out from the Olds Motor Works in Detroit and started East. He bounced over Canadian roads, followed Erie Canal towpaths through New York State and in seven-and-a-half days reached Manhattan. R. E. Olds greeted him warmly, and proceeded to exploit the news of the longest trip made by car in America.

The National Automobile Show was on. A. G. Spalding, the sporting goods house, approached to set up a New York agency, had turned Olds down on the grounds that selling 100 cars in New York was unlikely. But R. M. Owens of Cleveland jumped at the chance for a Manhattan agency. Olds signed him up for a 1,000 car contract. By a series of stunts, Owens made the curved dash Olds the most talked about car in New York, sold out his supply and soon announced a waiting list.

Now that Ranny Olds had a market, he needed production. He turned to John and Horace Dodge for transmission gears, to Henry M. Leland for engines and to Charles M. Mott for axles. In 1902 Oldsmobile achieved the sensational production of 2,500 cars, more than a fourth of the entire industry's output. The following year, Olds nearly doubled his output to become the undisputed leader in the low-priced field.

In 1904, when Olds' financial backers insisted that the company produce higher priced cars, Ranny Olds sold out his interests and resigned.

Under its new policy, Olds sales declined, and the company was languishing when General Motors bought it in 1910. Meantime, R. E. Olds organized a new company, REO, whose name was derived from his initials. The Dodge brothers, making a fortune by supplying Ford, later produced their own car. Leland became head of Cadillac and later Lincoln. Mott sold out to General Motors, largely for stock, and retired early as a multi-millionaire. Test driver Chapin deserted the towpaths for a managerial role with Chalmers, then helped organize the Hudson Motor Co. and in 1909 became its president. He attained political prominence as Secretary of Commerce in President Hoover's cabinet.

SUCCESS STORY

Roy D. Chapin, bounced out of Detroit in a curved-dash Oldsmobile. Well launched on the automotive ladder, he kept climbing. Eight years later, right, he had become one of motordom's first ranking citizens. Now flawlessly groomed, he drives a 1909 Hudson.

A.M.A.

EASTWARD HO!
Packard planned a spectacular stunt for 1903 — a motor trip from coast to coast. Tom Fetch was hired to drive "Old Pacific" eastward from San Francisco. After 53 torturous days, Fetch and his crew arrived in New York.

Packard Motor Co.

COAST TO COAST

First motorist to claim crossing the continent by car was Dr. H. Nelson Jackson, of Burlington, Vermont, driving a 20 h.p. Winton. Accompanied by his chauffeur, Sewall K. Crocker, and his bull dog "Bud", Dr. Jackson left San Francisco May 23, 1903 and arrived in New York July 26. Of the sixty-three days on the way, nineteen were spent waiting for the arrival of new tires or parts.

The doctor estimated he drove 5,600 miles, some of which represented wasted effort. Near Sacramento, a woman misdirected them by fifty-four miles in order that her family might get to see an automobile. At Silver Springs, Oregon, with the gasoline supply exhausted, chauffeur Crocker walked twenty-nine miles and rode three miles more on a bicycle to get five gallons of fuel. It cost him $25. At Granger, Wyoming, the Winton detoured sixty-nine miles to avoid a narrow ravine. A half dozen river crossings were made by bumping for miles along cross ties in order to use railroad bridges.

Ugly rumors spread after Dr Jackson's arrival home. It was whispered that he'd used two automobiles instead of one for the long journey. In some places he'd loaded his machine in freight cars for transportation across rough country, gossip held. Enraged at these rumors, the Winton Company posted a $10,000 reward to anyone who could prove either story. Dr. Jackson promptly added an equal sum. No money was collected.

Two other cars, a Packard and an Olds, made the coast-to-coast trek that year. To make sure that proper attention was accorded the Packard-sponsored exploit, the second continent conqueror, Tom Fetch, took along Marius C. Krarup, who combined the roles of mechanic, writer and photographer.

The scenery was grand, but passing was precarious for Fetch in mountain country.

The length of a canvas strip, left, provided the distance his car could travel in the Nevada sand. Right, Fetch built his own bridges as he proceeded.

As sales officials cheer, two Oldsmobiles get ready to leave New York on cross-country run to Portland. The cars arrived six weeks later.
A.M.A.

On June 18, 1903, they drove East out of San Francisco, groaned across the mountains, descended into Nevada. For seven days their car, "Old Pacific," crawled across barren waste. To get traction in the sand, Fetch laid down a strip of canvas. On other occasions, floor boards were removed from the steaming car to form the road ahead.

In Carson City, a crowd deserted the scene of a murder committed earlier in the day to watch the car chug through town. The Packard strained on through Utah, surmounted the Rockies and reached the Great Plains. Iowa proved a sea of gumbo. On one stretch "Old Pacific" sweated it out from 5:00 A.M. to 9:00 P.M., gained a meager twenty miles.

On the fifty-third day, Fetch and Krarup arose early in Poughkeepsie and headed for New York. Here a royal welcome awaited them. They were met at Yonkers by 200 enthusiastic motorists in fourteen cars, who escorted "Old Pacific" down Broadway to a West 59th Street garage in Manhattan. The occasion prompted Colonel Pardee, New York agent for Packard, to proclaim:

"This trip has proven that the automobile is a reliable means of locomotion and no longer the plaything of the rich."

The third coast-to-coast crew consisted of L. L. Whitman and E. J. Hammond, both of Pasadena, who made the trip in a 1903 Oldsmobile runabout. They took along a letter from Mayor Schmitz of San Francisco and after a leisurely journey delivered it to Mayor Low of New York.

In 1905 the Oldsmobile people decided upon another long-distance jaunt to promote the product, this one from New York to Portland, Oregon. For good measure they made it a race between two Olds, "Old Scout" and "Old Steady." The two cars started from New York on May 8 and arrived in Portland on June 21.

The following year, L. L. Whitman, at the wheel of a Franklin, drove from New York to San Francisco in fifteen days, two hours, fifteen minutes —a record. Transcontinental travel by now had become more commonplace.

The crew of "Old Scout" encounters vacationing schoolteachers in Wyoming, persuades the bolder ones to pose for a picture.

DAY AT THE FAIR
The automobile noisily grabbed publicity from other forms of transportation at the 1904 Louisiana Purchase Exposition. Among AAA tourists arriving from the East was a party headed by F. A. LaRoche, driving a famous French Darracq.

Ubiquitous cameramen have a field day inside Transportation Hall, left, where cars are contrasted with towering steam locomotive. Igorots from the Philippines, right, go by car through the Manila Gardens at St. Louis.

Group of White steamers ready to leave Vanderbilt home, Fifth Avenue and 58th Street, New York, for the St. Louis exposition.

MEET ME IN ST. LOUIS

Anything can happen at a World's Fair. The 1904 St. Louis Exposition was no exception. A dusty caravan of American and foreign cars showed up from the East, leaving behind a long trail of dead dogs, flattened fowl and indignant farmers.

At Erie, Pennsylvania, one driver reported he'd killed seven chickens in the course of a ninety-four mile run. Not so happy was Charles Glidden, who came along the route later and encountered a farmer with a loaded gun. Glidden forked over a dollar for each dead hen. Road routes each day were marked with confetti. When the supply ran out in Indiana, corn was used; fowl promptly flocked on the road, and wholesale carnage resulted.

Seventy cars had entered the tour to St. Louis, which the American Automobile Association sponsored. Fifty-eight cars actually arrived. It was the largest tour up to that time—1,264 miles of driving was involved for some contestants.

"The tour has taught the American public a great lesson," said the *Horseless Age*. "It has demonstrated beyond the possibility of a doubt that the cars built in this country can stand side by side with their foreign competitors."

Automobile Day at the fair was celebrated on Friday, August 12, 1904, with the AAA tourists accorded place of honor in a line of 300 machines. The parading automobiles rumbled through the 1,240 acre fairgrounds, attracting more attention than the woolly-headed Igorots from the Philippines.

EARTHQUAKE DUTY

A shattered municipal building provides background for photographer
Nick Lazarnick, who was rushed to San Francisco by a motor magazine on getting news of the 1906 earthquake. Shown in foreground is
a White Steamer awaiting emergency assignment from the military.

DISASTER SERVICE

Mayor Eugene E. Schmitz had every right to be pleased with his bus-
tling, prosperous city as he toured Golden Gate Park and environs on a
sunny Sunday afternoon, April 15, 1906. From his comfortable Pierce
Arrow, the Mayor's view of San Francisco's future had a glow as roseate
as the sunset over the Bay.

But within two days, his municipality was a shambles. Earthquake
rocked the Bay area at 5:15 A.M. Wednesday morning, and fire quickly
roared through the stricken metropolis. Five hundred thousand people were
homeless by Thursday. Fleeing the inferno, refugees by the thousands
dragged their bedding to Golden Gate Park. Flames destroyed three-fourths
of the city, wiped out virtually all communications, wrought destruction at
the rate of a thousand dollars a second. Transportation came to a standstill.
The only wheeled vehicle that moved around the streets was the automobile.

All available automobiles were pressed into service. They rushed the injured to hospitals, conveyed the infirm to safety, lugged dynamite to soldiers
endeavoring to check the flames. Tonneaus of fashionable cars were heaped
with bedding, household utensils and clothing salvaged from stricken
homes. Other cars sped through the debris, carrying messages between mili-

tary headquarters and stricken areas throughout the Bay region. A trade paper yapped: "Perhaps it will be less difficult now to secure a hearing among military powers-that-be. San Francisco opened a few eyes."

Hearing of the disaster, Walter C. White of the White Sewing Machine Company, of Cleveland, cut short his vacation and rushed up from Los Angeles in his White steamer car. On Friday, as he tried to enter San Francisco, a military sentry halted him at the barrier and promptly commandeered his car for emergency duties. As none of the available soldiers knew how to drive, White offered his services. They were promptly accepted. White was "on the go" day and night for several days with a soldier at his side to make sure he didn't chuck his assignment. As soon as he could get word back to Los Angeles, a caravan of White trucks were organized to carry supplies to San Francisco's victims. He became a local hero in another way, too.

Finding his company's garage at Market and Franklin Street completely destroyed, White acted decisively. In front of the ruins, he placed a large billboard proclaiming: "The new White Garage being erected on this site will be the FIRST AUTOMOBILE STATION IN THE WORLD." Public opinion responded favorably.

"The automobile has made a stride in public favor since last Wednesday morning which it could hardly have gained in years under ordinary conditions," observed one San Francisco newspaperman.

Automobile Topics editorialized:

"Hereafter the people of San Francisco will regard the automobile as a blessing, rather than a nuisance, as so many of them probably did previously."

Always alert to opportunities to kick the horse in the teeth, the publication observed that the automobiles performed a variety of jobs "without tiring or becoming frightened by the gruesome sights around them." Similarly, a San Francisco newspaper commented that "Horse flesh could never have stood the high pressure and could not have covered the immense distances encompassed by the motor-driven machines." The automobile came through the disaster with its reputation richly enhanced.

Army officer inspects the refugee camps at Fort Mason and Paccidi in a private car commandeered for the emergency.

A.M.A.

MAKING THE APPOINTED ROUNDS

First test mail collection by motor took place in Cleveland in 1899 under wintry conditions. A 9-h.p. Winton covered 22 miles of streets, stopped at 126 boxes and completed the route in two hours and 27 minutes. The time required for a horse-drawn wagon under favorable conditions was six hours.
A.M.A.

A LOAD OFF DOBBIN

The carriage trade was beginning to snub Dobbin; not so the tradesman. He found the horse a necessity to deliver his ice, groceries and dry goods around town. Yet here and there a motor truck appeared, doing the job a horse should do.

The origin of the truck is obscure. Winton introduced a Commercial Delivery Wagon in 1898. A Denver dry goods firm used Whites by the turn of the century. A few years later the *St. Louis Post-Dispatch* bought fourteen motor delivery wagons to replace fifty horsedrawn vehicles. Boston soon discovered it could deliver express to the suburbs at $4.50 a day per truck. A new trend in transportation had just begun.

A Winton truck made an experimental U. S. mail collection in Cleveland in 1899. The horse was shown up badly. The truck covered the twenty-two mile route in less than half the time the horse required for the same distance. Yet it took the Post Office fifteen years more to set up a motor vehicle division.

Early in the century Macy's speeded up their cross-town deliveries to the delight of housewives and urchins alike. American Express, right, determined by test the relative cost of motor vs. horse-drawn freight.

ROBUST ROAMER

The Rover Boy urge for outdoor adventure found full expression for the American male when he climbed behind the wheel of a car. In the golden years, 1905-15, touring rose to its zenith as a sport. America had become the pathfinder's rutted playground. Caravans of cars roamed the continent in the motoring season, competing for points, blasting the rural quietude and blazing rubber-tired trails across forlorn prairie country.

The motorists proved a sporty lot—debonair, swashbuckling, and often affluent. Farmers considered it fair game to gouge a hapless wayfarer mired at the roadside. Inn keepers tripled their rates when motorists registered. Constables delighted in penalizing minor infractions of the law. But this did not discourage the robust tourist. He was discovering America and enjoying it hugely.

Acknowledged king of the tourists was Charles J. Glidden, a retired Bostonian, financially independent from telephone pioneering. His motoring exploits bordered on the fabulous. Early in the century, he calmly set out to drive around the world in an English-made Napier. He took four years, traveled 46,528 miles, visited thirty-nine countries. An admirer exclaimed:

"What Columbus did for sailing, Charles J. Glidden did for motoring."

Accompanied by Mrs. Glidden and friends, he saw the Arctic on driving through northern Norway. In southern New Zealand, Glidden had a glimpse of the Antarctic. He even got into Tibet, the Forbidden Country. While Asiatic countries were regarded as "uncivilized," he found some good roads there, laid like a parquet floor.

On his return to America in 1905, the Bostonian launched the annual "reliability tours," popularly known as the Glidden tours.

AROUND THE WORLD BY CAR

Charles J. Glidden, a wealthy Bostonian, won fame as "King of the Tourists" by driving around the world by car. Accompanied by Mrs. Glidden, he drove a 16-h.p. English-made Napier 46,000 miles, visited 39 countries. When taking the Sultan of Sulu for a ride, the potentate tried to leap out when the Napier exceeded 4 m.p.h. By putting flanged wheels on his Napier, Glidden was able to use railroad tracks. In his world tour, he rolled from Minneapolis to the Pacific Coast in this fashion. This picture was taken at the St. Louis Exposition.

A.M.A.

THE PERILS OF JEAN

Jean Newton Cuneo, only woman contestant in the 1905 Glidden Tour, plunged into a Connecticut brook on her first day in the run to Bretton Woods, New Hampshire. Strong, willing men helped get her White steamer back on the road to Greenwich. While she placed low in the contest, Mrs. Cuneo gained masculine plaudits for her pluck and self-control.

TOURIST TROUBLES, 1905

Thirty-three cars competed for Charles J. Glidden's silver trophy in the first national road tour in 1905. The route—New York to Bretton Woods, New Hampshire—provided hills and dales aplenty, rough roads and steep grades.

Worse than terrain, however, was the attitude of the New England villagers. They strung ropes across the roads, nearly beheading the contestants. In passing through Leicester, Massachusetts, several contestants speeded their cars down the hill in order to gain enough momentum to climb the next hill. The town constable lay in wait and fined eight motorists $15 each for exceeding the town's 10 m.p.h. speed limit. Among other annoyances, grocery stores charged the tourists exorbitant gasoline prices, and hotels jacked their rates skyward.

Packard Motor Co.

A cool glass of buttermilk at the roadside helped soothe
the parched throat of the Glidden tourist. Car is a Packard.

Percy Pierce, driving a Pierce Arrow, was declared the winner from a
notable field that included R. E. Olds, Walter White and John D. Maxwell.

Most attention, however, was attracted by a woman, Mrs. John Cuneo
of Richmond Hill, Long Island, the only female contestant. She won top
laurels for nerve and daring.

On the first day out, she encountered near-disaster when her White
Steamer bore down on a stalled car at a narrow bridge near Greenwich,
Connecticut. Unable to stop her careening machine, Mrs. Cuneo crashed
through the bridge rail and plunged into Brothers Brook below. Road re-
pairmen quickly extricated her from beneath her car, and pulled the White
back onto the road. Without hesitation, she again took the wheel and
dashed along to join the procession at Hartford.

The vast hotel at Bretton Woods was a welcome sight for most contestants. One sighed wearily, "We breathe clouds of dust all day, and spend
the night trying to get it out of our eyes."

Journey's end for the first Glidden tour was the big hotel
at Bretton Woods, scene of postwar international monetary
conference, a third of a century later.

A.M.A.

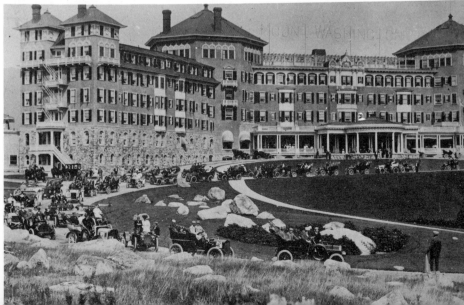

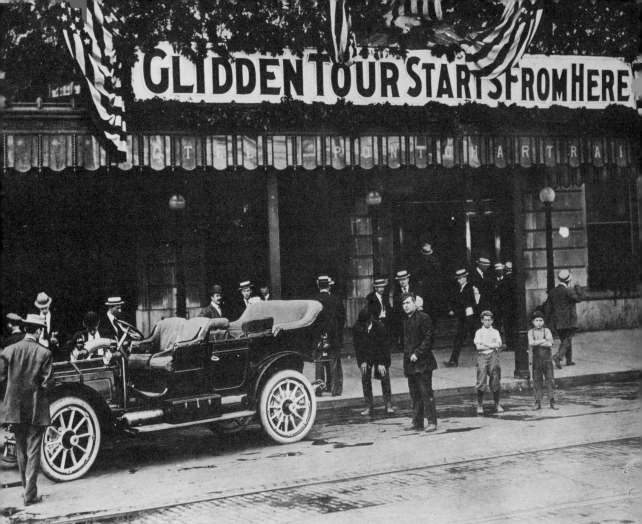

ROAD GOES WEST

Detroit's Pontchartrain Hotel, gathering place for motordom's notables, provided the start for the 1909 Glidden Tour. The route was an ambitious one — 2,640 miles. Destination: Denver.

WESTWARD HO!

The golden years of the Glidden Tours were from 1906 to 1911, when ardent motorists broke new trails with a pioneer's zest for discovery. The 1909 tour, perhaps the most ambitious of all, started from Detroit's Hotel Pontchartrain—fabled gathering place for industry notables—and went west to Denver.

Detroit gave the Gliddenites a rousing send-off. Some 1,030 motor vehicles, a fifth of them highly decorated, paraded the tourists around town. Such fanfare soon was discarded, however, when the tour got underway. In place of bunting, Gliddenites carried tow rope, axe, jack, and firearms for the trek across the open prairie. Coming up against fifteen degree grades, the tourist hitched tow ropes to stalled cars and hauled them up by hand.

Chuck holes in the prairie called for skill and patience.
Towrope, ax and shovel were required equipment for
Western trek.

Because of lack of hotels along the route, a special railroad train accompanied the tourist from Chicago well into the Midwest. By nightfall, the sleeping and dining cars were full of the trail-blazers, recounting the day's experiences. As they pushed further west, however, the comfortable rail facilities were left behind. The tour got down to a rugged basis. Sand storms, hail storms, gopher holes, chuck holes, mountain grades and other impediments to travel were encountered. But at last, they reached Denver, where a royal reception awaited. Then south to Colorado Springs, east to Salina and on to Kansas City, where the 2,640 mile tour ended. When the points were counted, Walter Winchester, a member of the Auto Club, had won. His car was the durable, powerful Pierce Arrow.

Driver of this Rapid Delivery truck got to know roads at
first hand.

41

Buffalo Motor Club

WHICH WAY TO DENVER?

A friendly farmer directs Dai H. Lewis, at wheel of an E-M-F, en route to Denver. The Buffalo Automobile Club manager laid out trails in the Spring and returned with Glidden cavalcade in Summer. On the Colorado prairie he had difficulty finding earlier wagon tracks which had guided him into Denver.

PATHFINDERS

Each spring a lone car, the AAA Pathfinder, ventured over soggy terrain to pick a route for the Glidden cavalcade to follow later in the summer. Adventure, tinged with adversity, invariably resulted.

The 1907 Pathfinder was a six cylinder Pierce Arrow assigned by the manufacturer, who had experimented with the model for over a year and believed it nearly perfect. The pathfinding job would uncover any defects if they existed, he was assured.

On a wet, disagreeable April day, with the roads a "sea of mud," car and crew set forth from Cleveland. Twenty-five miles west of the city the car's front wheel broke. Outside Indianapolis a few days later the frame cracked in two. Some miles later the cooling system began to boil. On removing the radiator cap, the frightened driver watched hot water spout to house-top height. Next went the exhaust pipe. Gamely the pathfinding crew plowed onward, plotted their route, then returned to its Buffalo factory a battered, bruised, groaning derelict on wheels. It had passed its test.

The pathfinding assignment required the patience of a roadside Job. The man who undertook it most frequently was a determined Welshman, Dai H. Lewis, manager of the Automobile Club of Buffalo. His most trying trip, Detroit to Denver, got started on April 12, 1909. With an E-M-F car as the Pathfinder, Lewis headed for Wisconsin, taking along a driver, a newspaperman and a photographer. Going from Madison to La Crosse they encountered a 154 mile stretch that required six consecutive days of travel. On it they paid farmers $200 in fees for extricating the car from clay and quick-

42

sand. At one point, it appeared that towing costs might sky rocket, for a farmer declined to help them unless they bought his team of horses.

"If you want to pay me $400, the team is yours, and I'll give you as much of my personal help as I can to get you out of that mess. But as long as I own these horses I wouldn't put them on that stretch of road at any price."

Three strong horses from the next town, after sinking to their bellies in the mud, finally pulled the E-M-F into town at a more modest $15.

Near Fort Morgan, Colorado, the pathfinders were whipped by a severe sand storm. The crew pulled the top over the car, put the side curtains in place, and tried to follow wagon tracks toward Denver. No roads, no markers, no people could be found on the prairie. Only rattlesnakes, prairie dogs, prairie owls. This posed a problem for Lewis in his pathfinder role. His compass would not work in the car. No landmarks could be found in the prairie land for guidance of the tourists coming along later. When the actual tour reached this 60-mile prairie stretch late in the summer, grass 18 inches high had sprung up, completely concealing the wagon tracks so visible in the spring. Undaunted, Lewis took a chance he could "guess which way." On delivering his Glidden charges safely into Denver before nightfall, the robust, Rabelaisian Lewis headed for the bar at the Brown Hotel. He downed twenty glasses of beer before satisfying his thirst.

Evidence of Puritanism in the Bible Belt amused the fun-loving Lewis. His own clubhouse at Buffalo had a sign posted: "You are not Allowed to Drink Liquor, Beer, or Wine on This Property—Unless You are Alone or with Someone." He frequently instructed the tour photographer, Bill Krohn, to get pictures along the route that indicated the prevalence of less liberal tendencies.

Customs in the hinterland provoked merriment among these Buffalo motorists, whose club back home imposed no similar restrictions. Dai H. Lewis, right, paid farmers $200 in towing charges on one stretch of road leading into La Crosse, Wisconsin. Six days' consecutive travel were required to travel 154 miles through clay and quicksand.

Buffalo Motor Club

GLOBE GIRDLERS

Start of the most ambitious race in the world, New York to Paris, took place from Times Square on February 12, 1908. Six cars entered and, surprisingly, half of them finished, including the two shown clearly above. To the right is the Protos, a ponderous German make, equipped with six separate gasoline tanks with total capacity of 176 gallons. Lt. Koeppen, its driver, managed to reach Paris ahead of the other contestants. Judges denied him first place, however, as he had incurred a 30-day penalty for avoiding a stretch of road in Western U. S. To the left is Italy's entry, the Zust, which placed third.

NEW YORK TO PARIS

On Lincoln's Birthday, 1908, a curious crowd of 250,000 people gaped at six cars about to undertake a "mad, impossible scheme"—a race from New York to Paris.

This astounding event, jointly sponsored by *The New York Times* and *Le Matin,* was chartered over a 22,000 mile course, through Alaska and Siberia.

At 11:00 A.M. the six cars—three French, one German, one Italian, one American—started hopefully toward Albany. Almost before leaving Westchester, the round-the-world tourists knew they were in for trouble. A thaw had set in, transforming a naturally unsatisfactory road into a quagmire. Most of the foreign contestants found they were overprepared. Quantities of stores that could have no possible value outside the Arctic circle burdened their cars. Reluctantly, they began to lighten the ballast.

A scant ninety-six miles up the pike, the first car quit. The French-made Sizaire-Naudin broke an axle. Its driver, unable to speak English, could find no American agency carrying a replacement unit.

As the remaining racers headed West, they ran into a snow storm. It increased in violence as they neared Chicago. Bucking the blizzard through Indiana, the four-cylinder Thomas Flyer covered only seven miles in fourteen hours of driving. Yet, the Thomas—America's only entry—maintained its lead. Close behind came Italy's Zust, "high of poop and low of stem, thundering broadsides across the snow waves." A powerful looking machine, the Zust carried a 30 h.p. engine under its green, white and blue bonnet. Built up from its dash was a metal and canvas shield to protect the driver. The Latins found they needed other protection as well. Near Spring Valley, Wyoming, the Zust crew was followed by a pack of timber wolves. The frenzied Italians claimed they shot twenty of the terrifying beasts, leaving in the trail $200 in pelts for ranchers to collect bounty funds on.

First into Colorado, the Thomas team used the Union Pacific right-of-way through the Aspen tunnel. A few days later the Zust crew showed up, demanding the same privilege. Solemn railroad officials pointed out that the Thomas Flyer had damaged the loose gravel ballast along the right-of-way, and denied further use of their property to the contestants. The Zust people filed a protest, and gloomily took the longer tedious route over the snow-covered mountains.

Stymied at Pocatello, Idaho, Lt. Koeppen, driver of the German team shipped his ponderous Protos into Seattle by railroad, thus avoiding a 1,100 mile stretch of uncertain road. The rules committee levied a 30 day penalty against the German for this action, but allowed him to remain in the race.

On the forty-second day out of New York, the Thomas Flyer swept into San Francisco, twelve days ahead of its nearest rival. The Zust, after floundering in Utah, reached the outskirts of Los Angeles. Here a jagged stump ripped open their gasoline tank and delayed their triumphal entry into the city. A reception committee of their countrymen mobbed the Italian team when they finally showed up, showered them with oranges, flowers and champagne.

The Thomas team put their car on the first boat to Valdez, Alaska. They expected to embark immediately for a dash across the trails and frozen rivers to Fairbanks, Nome and the tip of North America. But the seasoned sourdoughs snorted. Taking their visitor for a short sleigh ride over the intended route, they showed them that the narrow sleigh tracks wound through snowdrifts three to twelve feet high. Disillusioned, the American racers decided to re-ship to Seattle and take passage from there to Japan. Meanwhile the remaining contestants, apprised of the Alaskan conditions, already had sailed.

In the Orient, the world-girdling crew encountered other conditions that tried their souls. Bridges, virtually of toy construction, barely allowed passage of jinrikisha. The wide automobiles were forced to detour 200 miles to cover a ten mile stretch through the mountains. Arriving at Vladivostok, the Americans were dismayed to find that M. Saint Chaffrey had cornered all available gasoline for the French crews. For three days the Thomas men

A cold reception greeted this Italian crew, manning the Zust, when they first reached the West. Following a short-cut over the Rockies, they were chased off the right of way by railroad officials. In Wyoming, a pack of timber wolves panted after their chain-driven contraption. A jagged stump ripped their gasoline tank apart as they were about to make a triumphal entry into Los Angeles. Warm-hearted countrymen living in southern California provided them with a rip-roaring welcome, however, and tried to "drown them in champagne."

A.M.A.

American prestige took a big spurt forward when this Thomas Flyer, made in Buffalo, New York, was judged winner of the first global race. An ordinary stock model, this four-cylinder 60-h.p. car was picked from the regular factory supply six days before the race, officials claimed at race's end. They boasted it never had been in a garage. Mechanic George Miller and driver George Schuster took care of all repairs.
A.M.A.

fumed, then appealed to the American colony. An enterprising Yankee resident requested owners of launches to donate enough gasoline to allow their compatriots to get going again. Now behind the competition, the Thomas Flyer left Vladivostok on May 22, "struggling through endless stretches of mud, save where the road was lost in a pool of water, striking sunken logs and boulders, causing the car to bound up in the air and almost turn a complete somersault." Gallantly, the Americans pulled Lt. Koeppen out of a mud hole, and he in turn pulled out a bottle of wine to toast his rescuers. The race now narrowed down to the Protos, with Koeppen demonstrating real skill in driving, and the Thomas Flyer, with George Schuster at the wheel.

The Protos forged into the lead when the Thomas got lost in a Manchurian mountain maze. Then the two cars vied back and forth for the lead. It required seventy-two days for the Americans to cross Siberia, with only five nights spent in bed.

Slightly ahead as he left Asia, Koeppen kept his long Protos car out in front at Moscow, Berlin and into Paris. But the American team kept plugging on, and arrived in front of *Le Matin's* office in Paris on July 30, to the cry "*Vive le car Americain.*"

The Thomas car still had a margin in view of the thirty-day penalty levied against the Protos for its failure to get into Seattle under its own power. It was judged the winner. The only other car to finish was the Zust, which reached Paris two weeks behind the Thomas Flyer.

George Schuster and the other Thomas drivers had covered 12,116 miles in 112 days of actual driving. They averaged about 108 miles a day.

New York turned out en masse to welcome the winning team back, and President Roosevelt received them at the White House on August 20. The Thomas factory in Buffalo, hailing their make as "the most reliable car in the world," went on to assert that the race proved "that America leads the world in automobile construction by the same time margin that the Thomas Flyer led all comers of all nations in the great race around the world."

Chinese ox-cart

At this stage of the race the American car began to feel the re-sult of the commercial activities of G. Bourcier de Saint Chaffray, the conductor of the French De Dion car, who cornered the gasoline supply obtainable at Vladivostok and Harbin, with the exception of a small amount to be obtained by the Protos. However, upon appeal to the American residents of the city, a way out of the difficulty was found. A sufficient quantity was obtained from the

Chinese met on the plains of Manchuria

A.M.A.

A trade publication recounted the continent-by-continent progress of the Thomas Flyer.

OUTDOOR GIRL

The Gibson Girl, a soft, immaculate bit of feminine loveliness, gave way around 1908 to the Outdoor Girl. Mannishly garbed in Danish leather coat, cap and gauntlets, she raced her automobile down the road with wind beating against her tanned, toughened cheeks, rendering her nose a tomato-red color and scattering her hair like a witch's. Altogether she was an unlovely, disheveled sight.

A new feminine nightmare developed: "automobile wrinkles." Beauty doctors said that this condition—three deep lines between the eyes—came from the searching, concentrated gaze fixed on the road ahead. The sunlight's glare, added to this, produced a raw specimen for the beautician. In time, however, a home remedy was hit upon: rubbing the face with raw, freshly cut cucumbers.

Conscious of motoring's many hazards, the first women to drive wore their dingiest clothes—discarded dresses and bonnets, castoff shoes and other items from the attic. They were quickly weaned away from this unbecoming and niggardly practice. Fashionable tailors and modistes got busy, created a special motor garment. A fad was launched. Women who never intended to drive found it advantageous to wear a motor coat and veil; saleswomen gave them "far more polite attention when thus garbed," claimed the fashion arbiter for *Motor Print*.

The fair automobilist's ensemble was marred by the lack of effective wind-resisting headgear. Her cry to the milliners, reported *The Automobile*, was "Make me a hat that will stay firmly upon my head during a swift run and I will reward you with half of my pin money." The solution was found in a hat firmly affixed by a veil.

For sedate city driving, the wide, wind-resisting Cavalier hat could be exhibited by the female motorist. The car is an Anhut, model of 1910, with a carbide tank for its acetylene generator.
A.M.A.

"One of the most important accessories to the motor woman's toilette is the goggle; they are, of course, frankly ugly and unbecoming if not absolutely disfiguring, but like nearly all unpleasant things are exceedingly valuable," wrote one fashion arbiter.

A.M.A.

"No matter what the size of the hat, the veil should be three yards long and at least a half a yard wide," gravely intoned an auto fashion editor.

"As every woman knows, the first mission of the veil is to become the wearer and the second to protect the face and hair from dust and sun. To do this the back as well as the front of the head must be thoroughly covered while one is riding, but the gauze so arranged that it may be thrown aside quickly," the editor advised.

Not all women viewed the trend kindly. Mrs. A. Sherman Hitchcock of Providence, Rhode Island, an early woman driver and writer commented tartly: "The motorist of the fair sex might well be taken for a veiled woman of the East so completely is her head swathed in tulle and chiffon." On another occasion she observed, "They most closely resemble an Egyptian mummy."

In keeping with annual changes in car styles, fashion stylists, too, kept introducing new motor costumes. Women began to eschew the all-enveloping motor coat in favor of tailored mohair and serge garments, with striped skirts. When not in the car, they allowed their long veils to flow loosely down the back "precisely as does the conventional wedding veil."

The American woman began to strive for comfort, as she moved into an era of increasing freedom for her sex.

The same year the self-starter was installed, the first startling elevation of the lower hem of women's skirts took place, Mark Sullivan keenly observed. Women began to operate motor vehicles in greater numbers. And they began to discard their long petticoats and longer skirts, so that their feet would be free to work the pedals. Now in high gear, the American woman was striving for emancipation.

It proved a short step from the defiance-of-decorum scene above to the short skirt, women's suffrage, and feminine emancipation. Mark Sullivan observed that the first startling elevation of the lower hem of women's skirts took place the same year the self-starter was installed.

A.M.A.

CROSSROADS ENTERPRISER

Hanging out a new-type sign, the blacksmith began to cater to a new trade — the distraught motorist. Over his forge, broken automobile axles were mended. On his sawdust floor, ruptured tires were severed from their rims. The smithy began to repair mechanical deficiencies in cars, relieving the factory from dispatching a repairman to the scene. As manufacturers began to standardize on parts, the hometown mechanics took over the bulk of the maintenance job. Modern garages and service stations stemmed from such establishments as the one pictured here.

HOMETOWN SERVICE

When a mechanical failure occurred, a car often stayed put for weeks. On receiving reports of a breakdown, automobile factories frequently had to dispatch an all-around mechanic to the scene. A big forward step came in 1902 when royalties from the Selden patent were applied to an industry program aimed at developing part standards. Uniform sizes for screws, bolts, nuts, shafting, tubing and tires were agreed upon by an Association of Licensed Automobile Manufacturers technical committee. As the first decade advanced, motorists began to get service parts in their own communities, rather than writing back to the factory every time a breakdown occurred. Outside a few metropolitan areas, repair garages were unknown. But blacksmiths hung out their shingles (above) to acquire new business.

First full-fledged gasoline station in Flint, Michigan, occupied present-day site of Durant Hotel. This 1910 enterpriser sold filtered gasoline, thus saving the motorist the trouble of filtering his fuel through a chamois.

Motorists making long trips carried extra tins of gasoline and oil as these supplies were available only at an occasional grocery or hardware store. One auto editor gave this advice: "In the absence of gasoline, in a case where it is absolutely necessary, scout around for some kerosene. Most households have it, and drugstores carry ether. A mixture of two gallons of kerosene and a quart of ether may be rather expensive, but it will burn much like gasoline and require little carburetor adjustment."

Filling stations were slow to spring up. When they did, some city fathers viewed the fuel with suspicion. City ordinances forbade filling stations to keep on hand more than 250 gallons of gasoline. As late as 1913, a Canton, Ohio, operator took the matter to court, obtained permission to keep 1,000 gallons on his premises.

When valves leaked, motorist dropped nickel in slot and got a new one.
A.M.A.

Packard Motor Co.

Brown Bros

NO PLACE TO GO

No material improvement in road transportation resulted from Rameses II to President McKinley, insists automotive historian James Rood Doolittle. Rural roads proved impassable for months each year, and, at least, uncomfortable for the remainder. But the pressure for good roads was beginning to build up. Farmers, who had had no place to go, began to find the automobile an utilitarian device. In 1907 they put the power of their National Grange behind the good roads movement. The photograph left, taken a year later, illustrates road builders' efforts to find a satisfactory sub-base. Rock provided a sturdy but rough bottom to roads. The driver, right, of this 1907 Pope Hartford failed to find much improvement in road building even after McKinley.

ROUGH RIDING

In rural America, as in the White House, it was the age of the Rough Rider. The motorist venturing beyond city limits frequently found himself in country as backward as the Balkans.

Roads were regarded as being strictly in the local community's province. The farmer could avoid paying his road tax by laboring himself on the roads. Once a year he could show up with a team of horses, dump gravel in the chuck-holes, pack new dirt into the deepest ruts, fill in the washed-out areas and head home for early supper. With a shrug and a comment, "Well, that's out of the way for another year," he'd have dismissed his obligation.

The American type of road had a profound influence on car construction. At first, U. S. manufacturers strove to imitate the European prototype of vehicle. Then it became apparent that European car structures were unsuited for American roads. About 1905 American designers began turning out an uniquely rugged automotive design. Cars increased in size, weight, complexity and price. The gasoline car began to assert itself as the dominant type. Electric cars possessed limited range; steam cars continued to frighten prospective owners.

By 1907, farmers decided to get out of the mud and to join, through the National Grange, the good roads movement.

Undaunted by absence of bridge, this 1907 Packard tried to make the next bank, and failed.

Packard Motor Co.

Packard Motor Co.

ROADSIDE MANNER

Many a pleasurable ride into the country was marred by the failure of the pneumatic tire. Generally unreliable, this fabric-constructed tire contributed to motoring nuisances more than any other item on the car. One doctor estimated he spent $700 for tires alone in his first year of operation. Some motorists therefore went over to the solid tire, which detracted from the comfort but added to the reliability of motoring. The roadside scene above centers on a 1907 Packard, whose passengers are depicted in a characteristic pose of the period — manning the tire pump.

DOUBLE TROUBLE

Almost any car could take you places, cracked the wiseacres, but few would bring you back. As tires failed frequently, some car manufacturers did not include tires with their products. Instead they asked customers to make their own selection. This helped "take off the heat" when blow-outs and punctures occurred.

Antipathy of farmers toward motorists moderated somewhat when towing cars back to town produced profitable fees. One Sunday motorist, forced to detour from a well-traveled route, unexpectedly plunged into a deep, muddy hole. A farm boy rounded the bend with a team of horses, set his price—a stiff one—and with speed and dispatch extracted the motorist.

"Do you farm on Sundays around here?" inquired the motorist, as the boy prepared to leave.

"Nope, we just pull cars outta the hole."

"What do you do Saturday nights. Go out?"

"Nope," replied the youth. "Just haul water to the hole."

COSTUME PIECE

The fashion world moved in fast on a new market — styles for motorists. When invited for a ride, women in 1906 could truthfully announce that they "hadn't a thing to wear." The rigors of winter motoring made warm coats advisable. Brightly colored veils also were in vogue, as they both held big hats in place and afforded long, fluttering streamers to whip in the breeze. The people shown in the Packard car are models for a Detroit department store. This advertising photograph was taken in the summer, as the full foliage indicates, in preparation for the 1906 winter style season.

Roto

SNOWBIRDS

It was an age of change—both in cars and in motoring costumes. As cars became more durable, the motoring season was extended. This called for costumes nearly as furry as those that saw Perry through to the North Pole, and quite as expensive. Car prices were jumping, too, with a $7,500 average prevailing for most makes.

Engines were located in the rear on early cars. But designers soon began moving them forward. This was dictated by engineering considerations, principally weight distribution. As long as only a person or two went for a ride, weight was evenly distributed when passengers were seated in

This 1902 Haynes-Apperson Runabout, weighing only 1250 pounds, fared better in the snow than did heavier vehicles. The car cost $1200.

Albert Mecham

Going was rough in the Big City
in wintertime.
A.M.A.

the middle. When more began to ride, however, the engine was moved
forward to put added weight up front. This helped counterbalance rear
seat passengers, larger gasoline tanks and other weight factors.

Bodies became larger, heavier, sturdier. Alloy steels gradually were introduced, giving more strength and reducing weight. In 1904 headlamps
began to be included as standard equipment, an indication of the urge
of motorists to drive at night. The following year tire chains were introduced.

Winter motoring was rare, however. Most owners jacked up their cars
all winter long, and waited until the spring mud had dried up before taking their cars from the barn. But there always were an adventurous few
who attempted to drive under any conditions. They ventured forth despite
the roads, or absence of them. Their experiences hurried along automotive
improvements.

But it was rougher going in the
country.
Brown Bros.

ORIENTAL EXPRESS
En route to the peace conference at Portsmouth, N. H., in 1905, this Japanese delegation travels in a Pope Toledo car, famed for its high speed. Pleading that "progress of the world is being set back" by the Russo-Japanese war, President Theodore Roosevelt persuaded the two governments together to send delegates to a conference in the United States. The Treaty of Portsmouth, signed September 5, 1905, won for Roosevelt the Nobel Peace Prize, first ever awarded an American.
Brown Bros.

DIPLOMATIC IMMUNITY

Although wealthy Americans living in Washington drove foreign machines, the foreign diplomats of 1904 used American cars.

Despite their diplomatic choice of vehicles, some foreign dignitaries caused citizen's eyebrows to raise angrily because of the undiplomatic defiance of local traffic laws.

Immunity enjoyed by the diplomatic corps irked the District police, especially when the habitual speed violator from the Russian Embassy, Count Cassini, skirted about the Capital with his niece in a runabout. Not to be outdone, the ambassador's opposite number at the Japanese embassy, Kogoro Takahira, also purchased an electric runabout. As his country was at war with Russia, Takagira had to forego extended tours, but did manage to relax in the afternoons in drives to the city's edge. Next year his fellow countrymen used a gasoline car at Portsmouth, New Hampshire, where the peace terms were signed.

Pioneer diplomat-motorist of Washington was Turkish Ambassador Ali Ferronkh Bey, who learned to drive on the deserted grounds around the Washington monument. At an early period he managed to set his car on fire. This resulted not only in some personal injury but considerable damage to his prestige as a motorist. The incident did not dampen the diplomatic colony's zest for motoring, however.

The Chinese Ambassador caught the automobile fever and acquired a big touring car, which he proudly showed off to a visiting Chinese prince. On a long drive into the country, the car's cooling water gave out. No water could be found in the vicinity. It looked likely that the royal prince would have to be hauled ignominiously into Washington behind a mule team. In the nick of time, a milk wagon loomed up, and a deal was made to fill the water tank with milk.

A Washingtonian rides through Rock Creek Park in a hired car.

Ewing Galloway

Cigar-chewing Barney Oldfield symbolized to millions of Americans the phrase "mile-a-minute." His calculated recklessness and tremendous showmanship made him a great favorite with the fans.
A.M.A

SPEED CRAZY

America got madly excited about speed, speed records and speed demons. Every American boy wanted to "go like sixty." Father jammed against the railing at the county fair track to cheer his favorite daredevil, while inhaling dust and gasoline fumes. Mother went too, to show off her white dress, white hat and white parasol.

With the wane of hero worship for Admiral Dewey, a new national figure readily assumed his place. He was a jaunty, cigar-chewing, ex-bicycle rider named Barney Oldfield. In 1901, Henry Ford engaged him to drive "999," a four-cylinder, 80 h.p. red snorter in a ten mile race. It was scheduled at the Grosse Pointe track near Detroit. Oldfield learned to drive just before the event. Not knowing enough to slow down on curves, he kept "999" at full throttle and finished ahead of the field by an easy half mile. He kept up the pace for years.

The Empire City track at Yonkers, New York, became a mecca for Eastern sport fans with its "Mile a Minute Racing." When Barney Oldfield raced, the stands were filled to capacity. Let's look on as Oldfield performs at the track one summer day in 1903.

The crowd was on its feet when cars took the curves at top speed. To distribute the weight and keep the racer on even keel, the mechanic would grip the side handles and lean way out from the machine. The spectators, gasping at such recklessness, came back to the Empire City track at Yonkers in droves.

A.M.A.

All eyes are intent on the red Ford racer, being towed backwards into the straightaway. Nonchalantly seated in the racer is Barney Oldfield, clad in a red leather coat, bareheaded and with a half-smoked cigar in his mouth.

An announcer bellows out to the grandstands that Barney will try to better his own record for the mile, made on July 4 at Columbus, Ohio.

Back a third of a mile from the starting wire, Oldfield dismounts and turns over his engine with a long starting crank. Then he scrambles into his seat, an official dips a red flag, and with a rattle and a bang the racer gets underway. Barney steers diagonally across the turn and gets close to the outer fence for a long straight dash down the stretch. Before he gets to the wire, "999" is up to a mile-a-minute pace. He looks at the crowded grandstand, smiles broadly, and waves to the dusty gallery with his right hand. A murmur sweeps through the crowd.

Down the back stretch he flew bent low over his handles, and keeping close to the pole. He took the big turn at the opposite end of the course with a steady sweep and emerged again into the home straight. Watched breathlessly by every one, he cut diagonally across the track to the outside, this time smoothly and raising but little dust. As he shot for the second time down the homestretch, he leaned far out to the right apparently to measure his distance from the fence and the people lined up along it.

Once more the turn was taken diagonally and as the car slowed Oldfield was seen to bound several times in his seat. Anticipation of an accident rose to a high pitch, but old "999" quickly settled into her steady gait as the engine was throttled. Circling the track more slowly, Oldfield came to a stop in front of the grandstand, cigar still in his mouth and his face spattered with oil and dust.

The time announced for the mile was 55 4-5 seconds, a cut of three-fifths of a second from Oldfield's own world's record. Seven or eight newspaper photographers, with their big boxes, gathered and drove the crowding spectators back while hurried exposures were made on the intrepid hero of the day.

HOLIDAY THRILL
Auto racing became the new national sport. Fans flocked to the country-fair track on Fourth of July and Labor Day to watch the daredevils compete for gold and glory. Mile-a-minute speeds astounded the sports writers, acted as a magnet for the box office. The American vocabulary took on a new phrase, "Going like sixty." As the 1903 sporting editor might put it, the scalp-tingling thrill commenced when the starter sent his fuming charges roaring down the stretch at hair-raising speeds.
A.M.A.

When the crowd was finally quieted, the official announcer, through his megaphone, said: "I am requested by Oldfield to announce that he does not use Russian gasoline and would be pleased to meet any driver in the world; that he will go to the international race next year and that he won't be left at the post, either." Great applause.

Oldfield's exploits helped Ford gain national attention for his products, which was a factor in his sensational success. Years later, the billionaire manufacturer greeted his one-time driver with the remark:

"Well, Barney, I made you and you helped make me."

"Yes, Henry," the racing driver cracked back, "but I did a damned sight better job than you did."

AMERICAN CLASSIC

First of the races for the cup donated by William K. Vanderbilt, Jr. took place on Saturday, October 8, 1904, over a group of oil-laden roads, ordinarily accommodating public traffic, outside Westbury, Long Island. In three years it grew into the greatest sporting event in America. A crowd of 200,000 to 300,000 people came out to see "men whirl themselves in iron monsters over a dangerous country road at speeds faster than runaway locomotives."

Auto racing fans witnessed the Vanderbilt Cup Race with deadly intensity. The *Horseless Age* correspondents reported in 1904 that "over a pound of nails were picked up on a stretch not exceeding two miles near where we were stationed, showing the malicious intent to murder the contestants." In the 1910 event, a spectator hurled a bottle at the driver of a National as he flashed past. Instead, it struck his mechanic in the head, stunning him so that he almost toppled out of the speeding car. The driver held his teammate in his arm and finished the lap steering with one hand.

MILE-A-MINUTE
EXCITEMENT
On Long Island, Nassau County authorities permitted the public roads to be used for the Vanderbilt Cup races. This provoked considerable criticism, particularly as the $8-a-day Pinkerton patrols did little to control the spectators. Some hard-capped Pinkertons were hardly more than boys, such as the two in the left foreground. Others showed up half-drunk and paid scant attention to their duties.

A.M.A.

Mechanics suffered in other ways, too. In the initial race, driver and mechanic drew into Jericho to repair their Fiat. On starting up again, the mechanic tried to hop aboard, missed, and fell under the Fiat's wheels. In the same race, another driver hit a tree. His anxious mechanic hopped out to inspect the damage. Meanwhile, the driver hurriedly backed away from the tree trunk. Not seeing the crouched mechanic, he bowled him over before frantic yells stopped him.

Fate rode with the contestants. A stone thrown onto the course near Middlebrook by a reckless spectator probably saved the life of one driver. The stone bounded up from the road as Lewis Strang's tires hit the stretch, struck his radiator and promptly caused a leak. At the end of his lap, the furious driver pulled his car into the pits to stop the flow. Here mechanics found a more serious defect—a broken steering knuckle.

Fernan Gabriel, driver of a 90 h.p. Panhard, found that his pump chain had broken. Seeking to replace it, he reached for his supply box. Alas, its bottom had somehow jarred loose, and all his extra chains had been scattered along the route. That ended his participation in the contest which he'd been leading.

As early as 1904 one editor termed racing a menace. "The speed maniac is even now the great bane of automobiling, and the racing cult will simply multiply his kind and increase the nuisance," he predicted.

A favorite spot to visit during Vanderbilt Cup practice runs was the frame inn near Mineola, Long Island, which housed several of the American racing teams.

PHANTASMAGORIA

A weird, tumultuous, night scene, resembling phantasmagoria rather than reality, injected a nightmarish note into Long Island's autumnal mood. Automobiles from Brooklyn and New York, headlights aglare, horns a-tooting, weaved over the back roads, converging on Westbury. Trains unloaded at a country siding every half-hour spilling forth groggy groups of passengers. Car owners bidded spiritedly with Nassau county farmers for the privilege of parking by their fences. Parties of sportsmen, weary and bleary from a night at Rector's, scrambled for hard, cold grandstand seats.

Even with the dawn, the scene appeared fantastically dream-like. Tycoons and touts shivered side by side, trying to read postings on a score board. Venturesome souls draped themselves on telephone crossarms, and others perched squirrel-like in tree branches. Some camped out all night in tents, pitched at the roadside. A fortunate few, yawning from interrupted sleep, ambled along the course from nearby clapboard hotels, where they paid $100 a night for suites. The straightaway itself was black with spectators, who swung their arms to keep warm and jabbered excitedly about horsepower performances.

As developing daylight swept over the restless crowd, the $8-a-day Pinkerton patrolmen began to clear the course. The hubbub increased.

Above the din rose the throaty roar of motors, as begoggled drivers, American and foreign, warmed up their racing cars. The great American sports classic, the Vanderbilt Cup Race, was about to begin.

Exactly at one minute of six, Fred Wagner, the starter, signaled the contestants to get ready.

To the sound of a Gatling gun, the first driver let out his clutch and roared away to thunderous cheers. At the precise intervals of fifteen seconds, others followed.

The aroused crowd settled back to await their noisy return. The competing cars raced down the straightaway, followed public roads over a twenty-eight mile triangular course, with Queens, Jericho and Plain Edge as the corners.

Before the starting fumes wafted away, enterprising hucksters were noisily hawking their sandwiches up and down the road. A few wandering minstrels with guitars, banjos and harmonicas vied for favor. Three card monte and shell games got underway. "All fair and square," a blonde operator shouted, trying to entice newcomers to the tables.

At Krug's corner, a dangerous turn near Mineola, prosperous spectators paid heavily for the privilege of watching the race from their own car seats. Fabulous prices were charged for parking spaces at such intersections. Farmers, it was reported, made enough in one day to lift the mortgage.

The crowd along the course was in a carefree, even reckless, mood. Ingenious spectators came equipped with wire nippers and cut away the fastenings that barred them from the road. Others slipped a dollar or so to the Pinkerton patrolmen to let them through the wire fence.

People persisted in crossing and recrossing the road in defiance of danger. One driver jammed on his brakes so hard to avoid hitting a group of spectators, that he ripped and blew out both rear tires.

After the winner of a race was known, the spectators swarmed over the course, entirely beyond police control. Worse offenders were those who had come in cars. Anxious to get home once the winner was determined, they started driving down the course itself, heedless of remaining contestants. In view of such conditions, judges on one occasion frantically telephoned outlying points to hold all cars. The race was called off immediately to prevent slaughter of spectators.

DANGEROUS TURN
Wire fencing held back the crowd at the dangerous Krug's Corner turn. Farther up the road, however, spectators used wire nippers to get through the fastenings. One driver, skidding to avoid a group huddled in the road, blew out his two rear tires. Another contestant, John Tracy, driving a 90-h.p. Locomobile, turned into the North Hempstead Turnpike without slackening his pace and sent a drunken man rolling into the dust, unhurt.

A.M.A.

A new hoisting device, imported from Europe, stepped up the pace of the Vanderbilt by allowing drivers to change their tires quickly. When George Robertson won the 1908 race, he used a new demountable rim, which allowed him to hurry up tire-changing.

A.M.A.

YANKEE CHALLENGE

With aggravating regularity, European cars humbled American makes in racing. In commenting on the "miserable showing made by our representatives" in the Bennett Cup races of 1903, the *Louisville Courier-Journal* of July 4, 1903, said:

> None of them really expected to win the race, unless it be through the bad luck of cars of France or Germany, but it was thought that they'd do better than they did . . . France is at least five years ahead of the United States in the development of the automobile while Germany is not far behind France.

The Vanderbilt Cup race was intended by its founder to encourage American competition by establishing an international race on this side of the Atlantic.

In 1904, an American-born driver, George Heath, won the first Vanderbilt Cup race, but in a French-made Panhard, and wearing the colors of the Automobile Club of France. Another Frenchman came in second. The next year, France again took first and second place. In the third race, France scored its third consecutive victory and Italy took second place.

No race was held in 1907, owing to the inability to secure a properly guarded course. But the following year the patriotic American press was jubilant.

"America has at last come into her own. An American car, designed by an American, built by Americans in an American factory, of American material, and driven by an American, finally won America's classic contest in the fourth year of stubborn perseverance of Americans to place American cars in a speed level with the products of Europe," *The Automobile*, an American publication, reported.

George Robertson, a handsome, winsome New York City boy, only recently of voting age, drove a Locomobile to victory over eleven laps of a 23.46 mile course, averaging more than 64 miles per hour. His finish was one of the most dramatic in the history of the Vanderbilt Cup races.

On the seventh lap, Robertson took the lead. For the remaining laps he fought to keep it from Herbert Lytle in a Isotta, hitherto unbeaten in any road race that year. Robertson entered the last lap with a three minute, fifty second margin. Then the grandstands were thrown into a turmoil on the news that the Locomobile had stopped near Jericho on the backstretch.

It was tire trouble. While designer A. L. Riker and other backers in the stands chewed their nails, Robertson and his mechanic pitched into their task. The Locomobile had a new demountable rim. Miraculously, the tire was switched in one minute, forty-eight seconds. An announcer grabbed his megaphone and yelled the news to the seething crowd.

Lytle and his Isotta flashed by the stands, first to pass the post. Torturous minutes of waiting followed. Watches were out. Anxious eyes scanned the hill up the stretch. "I'd give five hundred dollars to see that American car win," said Henry Ford, an excited spectator.

Robertson had started ten minutes after Lytle and had that margin in which to finish. Five, six, seven minutes passed. No Robertson. Eight minutes, and "a mighty shout went up" as the big radiator of the Locomobile showed itself over the hilltop. It took but seconds for Robertson to dash down the homestretch and across the tape—winner.

HENRY FORD—PROTAGONIST

At forty, Henry Ford was a near failure. With two attempts to crash the auto game behind him, he tried again in June, 1903, when Ford Motor Company was organized with $28,500 capital. Chauncey M. Depew talked his nephew out of a fortune by advising him against investing $5,000 in Ford's business, observing that "the horseless carriage will never supplant the horse." In 1904, Ford's most popular model sold for $900 (advertisement below) but one group of stockholders urged that company invade the high-price market. Ford favored staying in low price field, and in the resulting controversy, some stockholders sold out. Ford, who'd been drawing a $300 a month salary as vice president and chief engineer, in 1906 emerged with controlling interest in the company. Boss at last, he was free to pursue his own policies. He faced a rocky road, however, as his company was being sued for infringement of the Selden Patent, which covered the use of gasoline engines for automobiles.

The box in Ford's advertisement utters his defiance of the group of companies controlling the Selden patent. Reference to "Always a Winner" was Ford's attempt to capitalize upon his racing exploits. Ford raced his early cars himself, and bested Alexander Winton, the Cleveland car manufacturer, in a heated 10-mile race at the Grosse Pointe dirt track in 1903. Later he engaged Barney Oldfield to drive for him.

A.M.A.

CONFIDENT WARRIOR
Henry Ford gained control of
his company in 1906 when several initial backers, skeptical of
his "crazy" ideas, bowed out.
Ford decided to abandon the
big car field to others, and to
concentrate on a low-cost universal car. He is seen above in
front of his Broadway salesroom
in a model which preceded his
famous model T.
A.M.A.

GEORGE B. SELDEN—ANTAGONIST

A shrewd Rochester attorney, George B. Selden, saw an European
model gasoline engine at Philadelphia Centennial in 1876. He soon filed a
patent application for a gasoline engine, nursed it along for years. In 1903,
a group of car manufacturers, licensed to use gasoline engines, sued Ford
for patent infringements, and a long, fierce legal battle began.

Not until December 24, 1906 did Selden officially enter the automobile
business, by incorporating the Selden Motor Vehicle Company. He announced plans to build at East Rochester, New York, a touring car to sell
for about $5,000 and, in time, to add a line of commercial vehicles.
Throughout 1906 an odd situation prevailed; inventor Selden was unable
to manufacture under his own patent. The Association of Licensed
Automobile Manufacturers, controlling the Selden patent, had ruled that
no license should be granted until the applicant had demonstrated his
ability to manufacture automobiles of the standard required and had actually sold some of them. The license, refused when the Selden company
was in its promotion stage, finally was granted near the year-end.

In 1908, Selden and his sons built a model which they demonstrated
for the court. Selden's patent was ruled invalid in 1911. A diary entry
revealed that years before, he'd scorned the four-cycle Otto engine as
"that damn Dutch engine" in favor of the two-cycle Brayton engine, which
only one car being made in 1911 was using.

In 1908 George B. Selden and
his sons built this model — the
first car he ever actually had
made. In 1911, Selden's patent
was ruled valid, but not infringed by Ford and other non-
licensed manufacturers.
A.M.A.

Packard Motor Co.

One day's production of Packard cars leaves the plant for test run. Each car was road-tested before being shipped to dealers and customers.

GOOD OLD DAYS

"Detroit, the Beautiful," once a sleepy, tree-lined town, began to burst its community britches. At the downtown Pontchartrain bar, new automobile promotion schemes were projected daily. Factory space brought premium rates. Parts peddlers arrived on nearly every train. Farmers from nearby communities took jobs as factory hands. Why not? The pay was good—$12.40 for a fifty-five hour week.

Detroit had adopted as its slogan "the city where life is worth living." Living was, at least, inexpensive. Bacon cost only ten cents a pound at the grocery, butter twenty-three cents. Father paid only $15 for his wool Sunday suit. A pair of shoes set him back $3.50. He could rent a seven room house for his family for $14 a month.

The Packard body shop in 1910 illustrated the handwork methods then prevailing. Building of car bodies was slow, tedious, painstaking work. Making the body alone cost more than today's entire automobile.

Packard Motor Co.

Like other Detroit factory workers, Packard employees rode the streetcars. Their wages averaged $12.40 a week. The automobiles they helped build cost $5,000 or more.
Packard Motor Co.

The city, also, was beginning to gain recognition as the Number One automobile center. Packard bought a forty acre farm off East Grand Boulevard, then the city limits and a "whiz course" for buggy and auto driving on Sundays. The conservative element in the community wagged their heads at the decision to build a factory in the cow pastures. They chortled anew as the structure began to rise. It was built of fine finished brick and reinforced concrete. Front windows were dolled up with awnings. Side and back windows were so closely spaced they gave the appearance of solid sheets of glass. Sunlight flowed in. The dirty, dingy appearance of the usual factory was missing. Skeptics shook their heads and asked, "Why try to make a factory look like anything but a factory?" Albert Kahn, then a promising young architect, had given Detroit the first of America's modern factories.

The workers responded well to the environment, and Packard began a long era of fine relations with employes. Band concerts enlivened the noon hour. Company picnics were held on nearby Belle Isle. Tennis courts were laid out alongside the plant for workers' use. The era of good feeling between management and workers continued for thirty years.

PLEASANT NOTE
Packard early gained a reputation for being a good place to work. Employee tennis courts adjoined the factory. Workers flocked to company-sponsored picnics and band concerts. Girls of the Packard accounting department, above, competed for prizes at the company's picnic on Belle Isle in 1906.

Packard Motor Co.

Traffic Safety Association
Of Detroit

In 1909 Detroit established its Traffic Division. When a car driver failed to stop for the policeman's hand signal, the officer was expected to chase after him. Most uninstructed drivers drove right past the traffic cops.

Few Detroiters rode in the automobiles they helped build. Streetcar lines were extended farther into the outskirts. Most everyone rode the trolleys to work. Bicycle riding provided great sport on Sundays. Not until 1909 did enough automobiles ply the streets to warrant creation of a Traffic Division. Then the city limited it to a sergeant and twelve patrolmen.

Four officers were stationed at Woodward and State, smack in the middle of downtown, and began to regulate traffic. A patrolman's upraised hand signaled "Stop"; by swinging his hands across his body, he instructed cars to "Go." The police commissioner instructed the officers to wear white gloves so they could be more easily seen. The citizens snorted, accused the commissioner of pretentiousness.

Not until 1914 did Detroit install its first stop signal which the Automobile Club payed for. City Hall officials said they didn't have any money for such nonsense.

MARK TWAIN ON WAR

Mark Twain, in the period when the champion of the strenuous life, Teddy Roosevelt, was riding high, told an audience: "I would have been a Rough-Rider if I could have gone to war on an automobile — but not a horse . . . There is no place where a horse is comfortable." Young man in bowler is automotive publicist, Worth Colwell. They are shown riding in a 1907 Dragon in Central Park.

A.M.A.

NEW YEAR DAWNS

New Year's, 1907, broke over New York City in a heavy fog. Celebrants huddled under umbrellas along Broadway. Times Square was shrouded in gloom. The political atmosphere, too, was thick.

"The country is now entering upon an era drifting toward a larger measure of state socialism," a government official in Washington was quoted as saying:

> *The New York Times* in its January 1st editorial warned: Mr. Roosevelt cannot press much further his recommendations of an income tax and inheritance taxes intended to put a check upon the transmission of great fortunes.

Wages and living costs were up. Russia was experiencing "a dark year." The United States intervened in Cuba. Perry attempted to reach the Pole.

Mark Twain's antics provided page one amusement for newspaper readers. On New Year's Eve, at a party at his sister's home, 21 Fifth Avenue, he pretended to get drunk and deliver a temperance lecture at the same time.

Joe Tracy, who had chalked up the fastest single lap in the Vanderbilt Cup race, started at 12:01 A.M. on a New York to Philadelphia run, using alcohol for fuel. A new act, which removed a stiff revenue duty on industrial alcohol went into effect at the exact moment of his departure. His car consumed thirteen gallons of denatured alcohol on the 100 mile run. Under the old law, the fuel would have cost $35.10. With the tax off, the trip cost $7.15. By using gasoline instead, Joe Tracy could have made Philadelphia on about six gallons, costing $1.20.

Mayor George B. McClellan's car is parked in front of his residence. Asked in 1907 to do something about New York's traffic tangle involving automobiles, horses and wagons, the mayor uttered a remark that has become an American classic: "Let's have a survey." Since that time, every New York mayor has used the same technique.

Brown Bros.

The automobile industry was breaking all records, doing $80,000,000 of business. Eastern factories were operating at full capacity. Foreign exhibitors, too, did well with their cars, priced between $3,500 and $13,000.

Motor industry spokesmen at a year-end dinner at Reisenweber's, observed "the sentiment against automobiles as such is dying out."

Loud grumbling reached Mayor George B. McClellan's ears, however, because of the growing traffic tangles in New York City. When public pressure was put on, the mayor hesitated only momentarily before coming up with an answer. "Let's have a survey," said the mayor, a car owner himself. The political heat subsided. The traffic congestion continued.

The seventh annual automobile show opened in Madison Square Garden in January with 150 different models presented. A dozen foreign makes, direct from the Paris Salon, gained exhibit space.

"The pre-eminence of the foreign engineer in the past has been a fact denied rather than disapproved, but now the proof is crowding close on the heels of the statement, and it is clear that the cars for the Garden Show are fully capable of price, style, finish, reliability, quality, or any other kind of competition with their imported competitors," a magazine writer observed.

The trend toward luxuriousness in American makes was noticeable in the more expensive body work and upholstery. Ornamental tool and battery boxes adorned the running boards. Leather pockets provided space for maps in the upholstery. Foot rests gave tonneau passengers a touch of elegant comfort. Hampers for picnicking were clamped on rear platforms.

The public paid the price—with higher prices. In 1907, average prices of American cars rose to $2,841, compared to $2,468 in the previous year and $2,127 in 1905.

"Even at this late day," pontificated C. B. Hayward in the January 10, 1907 issue of *The Automobile*, "there is the usual crop of ante-show prophecies about automobiles being vastly cheaper, and the arrival of the 'poor man's' car. In view of the present widespread state of education concerning things automotive that prevails, it is hardly probable that many people are deceived by talk of this kind. . ."

Robert W. Goelet, one of New York's wealthiest men, preferred driving French cars. He's at the wheel of a chain-driven Delauncey-Belleville. Mrs. Goelet supported the woman suffrage movement of the period. Cars began to get bigger, more luxurious, more expensive. Right, this six-cylinder Lozier Briarcliff sold for $6,000. It had a 131-inch wheelbase, possessed 51 horsepower. While the owner drove, the chauffeur rode the bucket seat.

AWAY TO CONEY ISLAND OUTING
Through Manhattan's street, the Orphans Day caravan had the right-away. In June, the automobile clubs in the metropolitan area rounded up private cars, commercial vehicles, and a Fifth Avenue bus to take the orphans to a Coney Island outing. The event was conceived by "Senator" W. J. Wagner, well-known promoter of racing meets and hill climbs. It became a yearly feature in New York, and inspired a wave of similar outings throughout the nation.

A.M.A.

DAY AT DREAMLAND

A softer side to the Big City showed up. One June morning in 1907, a caravan of 147 motor vehicles, brimming with orphans, headed for Coney Island. There the joys of Dreamland awaited—everything free all day.

Motorists donated their cars for the day. They lined up at 8:00 A.M., June 12, in front of the Charles M. Schwab residence, Seventy-third Street at Riverside Drive, and with mounted police in front headed down Broadway to the Brooklyn Bridge.

One car had a puncture. Before tears could flow, a motor scout scurried down the line and returned with two empty reserve cars into which the youngsters were transferred. Six commercial vehicles joined the parade. A big Berliet hauled a valuable consignment—1,200 boxes of candy.

On Long Island, a similar assembly of eight hundred orphans also headed for Dreamland, and the wonderous world of airships, shooting the chutes, the Bay of Naples, miniature Switzerland, Kansas Cyclone and the Days of Forty-nine. The candy disappeared like ice under a summer sun.

At five o'clock, the day at Dreamland came to an end. The children scrambled into the automobiles for the drive back. The day was considered a success—no injuries, no accidents, no mishaps of any kind.

"The car hasn't a scratch on it," said the owner of a new touring car. "I never saw a better behaved set of children. They shall certainly have my machine next year."

The leader of the band turns to get the signal from Samuel A. Miles, chairman of the 1907 event, before swinging his group into "Sidewalks of New York."

A.M.A.

CHEAPER THAN A HORSE
In an advertisement about its 1910 model, the Brush Runabout Company asked: "How many thousand times have you heard the expression, 'When they get a reliable automobile down to the cost of a good horse and buggy, I'll buy one'? Here it is! A car for less than $500." Not content to undercut the horse, the Brush also undersold Ford's Model T by $465.
Bettman Archive

BRAVE FRONT

A brave front characterized the Detroit car manufacturer. Never one to *under*estimate his product, he rarely failed to *over*state his expectations of its saleability.

"Before the next twelve months, Detroit manufacturers confidentially expect they will have produced 50,000 machines," reported the Michigan correspondent of *The Automobile* in December, 1908. This total, he explained, comprised as many automobiles as were made from 1900 through 1908.

"Owing to the unprecedented figures of production planned . . . a general impression has gone abroad that Detroit interests have enlisted the services of a skilled press agent and are talking 'big' mainly for purposes of publication," the correspondent continued.

The writer gave a special nod, however, to one Detroit engineer, who had just dropped his series of expensive makes and decided to concentrate on only one line, the Model T.

"After an interview with Henry Ford, one expects to see automobiles as common as building blocks upon getting out in the street, and in the vicinity of the Ford plant the expectation comes near being realized," the reporter commented.

Ford thought he alone would make 25,000 cars in 1909. Actually he came close to reaching his estimated goal. The year before, with dictatorial firmness, he had rammed down his associates' throats the concept of an "universal" car, announced that he'd build only one model, with the same chassis for all cars, and "any customer can have a car painted any color he wants so long as it is black." He built 19,051 of the Model T's in 1909 to lead the industry in production and sales.

The 1910 Brush, known as "Everyman's Car," looked like the better buy to some motorists. It sold for $485, nearly half the price of the Ford. Unlike the Ford, it was licensed under the Selden patent.

The Brush had a good record. It had finished in the 1909 Glidden Tour, rolling up 2,636 miles in fifteen days. It had climbed Pike's Peak

Brush Runabout driver calls on the Detroit *Free Press* to see about some publicity. A rival paper, the Detroit *News*, used two Brushes as messenger cars.

under its own power. It had crossed the American continent. In a 1909 test in Buffalo, the Brush made 41.2 miles on a gallon of gasoline—a fuel cost of less than ⅜th of a cent a mile.

Brush, too, decided to give his customers any color they wanted, so long as it was maroon. In 1912, the company became a division of the United States Motor Company, reduced the price of its Liberty-Brush runabout to $350 "to present new opportunities and advantages to millions of people." However, the Brush soon lost its identity, vanished from the American scene.

The Maxwell gave American motorists another good choice in the low price class. It sold for $600. Designed by John D. Maxwell, one of Elwood Haynes' original helpers, production of the car was financially backed by Benjamin Briscoe, who enjoyed Wall Street's confidence. The name of Maxwell continued to survive under several corporate auspices until 1925 when it was absorbed by Chrysler.

Flint, too, reached out for the low price market. A natty, four-cylinder Buick runabout, selling for $900, dazzled onlookers with its white enamel. Its mechanical qualities caused a dealer proudly to proclaim, "You can't hear her run in the street."

The Model T, however, kept chugging straight into the heart of motoring America. Having gained leadership in the industry, Ford kept it for the next seventeen years. In that time he produced and sold 15,000,000 Model T's. In some years he accounted for more than half of the entire industry's production.

On June 1, 1909, President Taft pressed golden telegraph key in Washington, Manhattan's Mayor McClelland fired a gold revolver, and away sped five drivers for the West Coast, 4,000 miles away. Ford's car reached Seattle first.

ROUGH RIDER'S RIDE

Lansing, Michigan, was more than ordinarily excited early in June, 1907, when President Theodore Roosevelt arrived for a visit. Two local companies, Reo and Olds, became rivals for the honor of transporting the President. By compromise, one car conveyed the President to Michigan State College, while the other brought him back. R. E. Olds is shown driving Roosevelt and his Lansing hosts.
Brown Bros.

POLITICAL PROGRESS

The decade's leading advocate of the strenuous life, President Theodore Roosevelt, kept automobiles pretty much at arm's length. Only a single automobile, a White, was permitted in his 1905 inaugural parade. Roosevelt himself rode in a horse-driven carriage. Not until Harding's inauguration in 1921 did the motor car become the accepted mode of conveyance for American presidential inaugurals.

The White House Secret Service detail looked upon the motor car with a jaundiced eye. Secret Service chief Edward Starling was particularly zealous in keeping the White House occupant out of automobiles. However, in 1929, in arranging for President Hoover's visit to Dearborn, Michigan, he turned thumbs down on plans for the President to ride behind a horse on the grounds "it is too dangerous." In insisting that Hoover ride in a car, he grinned and recalled, "I remember one time forbidding President Theodore Roosevelt to ride in an automobile for the same reason—too dangerous."

"Teddy" Roosevelt consistently refrained from purchasing a motor car for the White House stables. Not until 1907 did he ride in an automobile publicly. A visit to Lansing, Michigan—home of both the Olds and Reo companies—provided the occasion. The rival firms fought bitterly over the honor of transporting the President from the station to Michigan State College, on the outskirts of the state capital. Finally the matter was settled by compromise. Reo took him from the station to the campus for a speech, and Olds brought him back. Reo showed one bit of enterprise. The company rushed out from New York ace photographer Nick Lazarnick, who took a picture of the President riding with R. E. Olds in his new make. The photograph was widely used in the nation's press.

President William Howard Taft, shown in rear seat, brought the first automobile to the White House. To avoid offending any manufacturer by making a personal choice of a car, he asked the War Department to ask for bids.

A.M.A.

President William Howard Taft, fond of riding in automobiles, asked the War Department to select two cars for his use after his inaugural. Manufacturers bid spiritedly for the privilege of furnishing the car. The White Steamer won out.

Before he reached the White House, Woodrow Wilson bitterly blasted automobiles. By 1912, he'd learned to enjoy automobiles. He selected Pierce-Arrows, with highly shined brass, for White House use.

Politicians early learned the value of automobiles in campaigning. *Horseless Age* recorded in 1905 that "the automobile is proving a great boon to candidates." The publication called attention to a district organizer in New York who covered sixty-six miles and visited all five boroughs in less than twelve hours. Another candidate, using an automobile, addressed five to ten meetings every night.

"It is to be hoped that the successful candidates will appreciate the services rendered them by the auto in their campaign, and during their term in office will show themselves favorably inclined toward the automobile movement," commented the publication.

President Woodrow Wilson, who had blasted out in 1906 that "nothing has spread the socialistic feeling in this country more than the automobile," by 1911 had grown fond of automobiles. He is posing above with a Cadillac car at Princeton, New Jersey.

A.M.A.

ELKS' HIGHJINKS

The 1910 Elks' Convention in Hutchinson, Kansas, featured a procession of automobiles, some featuring antlers on headlamps. The prairie states sported the less expensive, lighter cars made in American factories. New York, below, still was a big market for heavy, expensive, imported automobiles. The chauffeur was more apt to be found at the wheel than the owner, particularly on "state occasions," such as the Easter Parade.

Chapter 2

AMERICA IN TRANSITION — 1911-1918

CHANGING DAYS

THE AUTO INDUSTRY was beginning to grow up. A tinge of respectability at least was evidenced by 1911. For the first time, the New York Stock Exchange listed automotive securities. Competitors ceased their bitter tirades against each other in the nation's press. Ended at last was the litigation over the Selden patent, which had reached a point where the Licensing Association threatened to sue even the buyers of Ford cars. (The Court of Appeals held that the patent was valid, but that Ford had not infringed it.) Free of the costly litigation, the jubilant Ford scarcely took notice of the news of a newly organized Flint concern, the Chevrolet Motor Company of Michigan.

The year 1911 proved notable in other respects. Cadillac adopted Charles F. Kettering's electric starting device. The first rear view mirror was introduced. Studebaker discontinued electrics to concentrate on gasoline cars. General Motors Truck was formed, and so was International Motor Company, later known as Mack Truck. The first 500-mile speedway race was run at Indianapolis. And the industry enjoyed a record production year of nearly 200,000 passenger cars, and 10,700 trucks and buses.

In some respects, though, motoring began to lose some of its charm and distinctive flavor. The special costumes for automobilists began to go out of style. The patrician strain of the knights of the road became diluted. Plebeian drivers of Fords, Brushes, Maxwells began to outnumber the old motoring aristocracy. The Elks Convention in Hutchinson, Kansas, could put as many cars on display as Newport at the height of the summer season. Mid-America became a growing market for automobiles. Here the preference was for U. S.-made products rather than the imported models. A decided break was made with the European tradition of the right hand drive—several American manufacturers began to install steering mechanisms on the left hand side. Soon a profusion of both right and left hand drives could be spotted on the parking lots at major sporting meets.

ON THE FENCE
A few years after this 1910 photo was taken, the fence-sitters would smile at themselves. Their elaborate, expensive costumes went out of fashion quickly after the end of the century's first decade. Automobile ownership no longer became the mark of conspicuous wealth, and the motorist no longer dressed to the goggles for the part. In the second decade, the automobile's influence was being exerted on the whole national culture, and its effect on fashions soon took another turn — toward shorter skirts.

A.M.A.

The multi-million-dollar research laboratory for motor development scarcely was a glint in Charles F. Kettering's eye in 1913. Here he's conducting on-the-spot research with a test Buick.
General Motors

SELF-STARTER

A homely, homespun Dayton revolutionist with a monkey wrench in 1911 created a greater change: Charles Franklin Kettering eliminated the crank.

Starting a car had long been a discouraging, frequently dangerous task. Across the nation, the backfiring of engines produced a bumper crop of gashed hands and broken arms. And when an automobile engine was carelessly left in gear, the hapless motorist often experienced more serious injury.

Henry Leland, head of Cadillac, was still brooding over the death of a friend, who had sustained fatal injury while cranking his stalled Cadillac, when Charles Kettering approached him with his self-starting device. The thirty-four year old inventor walked off with an order for four thousand starters for Cadillac.

The bankers running General Motors heard of Leland's extravagant commitment. Their electrical engineering experts insisted the device could not work. Before a frozen-faced audience one February morning in 1911, Leland got behind the wheel of a Cadillac with a newly installed Delco starter.

The white-bearded Leland adjusted the spark, turned the switch and pressed the button. The engine roared. Leland then advanced the spark, reduced the gasoline intake, and let the engine drone steadily with power. The initial gamble was won, and with it more important stakes were acquired—the confidence of millions of women in motoring.

MOVING ASSEMBLY

Henry Ford's new plant at Highland Park, a Detroit suburb, developed into a proving ground for industrial mechanization. The restless-minded inventor gave associates full rein to experiment on ways of taking the work to the men, instead of shifting men from task to task.

Initially, gravity chutes were used to slide auto parts to the workmen. Even Ford bodies slid down an incline plane to the crude Ford assembly line.

Not fully satisfied, Ford technicians kept improvising. Dry goods stores had successfully speeded merchandise overhead in trolley baskets. Meat packers had shoved carcasses along to dressers via a moving trolley. Ford's specialists took all such ideas, stirred them up, and brought forth new applications of material handling.

Ford's engineers broke down the assembly line into separate operations, assigned one man to each, then speeded the parts to him by mechanical conveyor. Inching forward with their experimentation, they arrived at the point where the moving assembly technique could be applied to the final job.

The moving final assembly line was born in the summer of 1913 when a car was assembled while in continuous motion. It had taken more than twelve hours to put together a Ford car. With the installation of endless belts and overhead conveyors, the time was shaved to ninety-three minutes.

The revolution was on. Ford production attained the incredible rate of a thousand cars a day. He had become the undisputed leader of the automobile industry.

Gravity chutes, used in a Lowell, Massachusetts, dry goods store in the 1870's for getting sales slips to the cashier's cage, provided inspiration for Ford. His workmen in early 1913 found the method helpful to get a car body on a Model-T chassis. A few months later, they took a cue from the Chicago meat packers and installed a moving conveyor, similar to those that carried carcasses in a slaughterhouse. Before the close of 1913, Ford's output was more than one third of the output of the entire industry.

Mary Pickford sported a Maxwell, long before Jack Benny. Below, a nautical note is infused into motoring. Wire wheels and sweeping fenders add a chic air to the car, matched only by the sophisticated manner of the driver.

Women dreaded cranking the car, perhaps not only because of its dangers but also because of its posture.

A.M.A.

WOMEN BEHIND THE WHEEL

"Should a woman doctor use an automobile or a horse?" Kate Campbell Mead, M.D. asked in a 1905 magazine article.

She gave readers the answer promptly:

> My answer comes at once: an automobile. Any ordinarily bright woman who can afford to buy a one-cylinder gasoline machine, or electric runabout, and can keep it on her own premises, can learn to manage it herself.

Posed a decade later, Dr. Campbell's question would have sounded quaint. By then women doctors, lawyers, Indian princesses and all manner of females, career-minded or domesticated, had swept forth from home, office and tepee to assume their rightful place behind the wheel.

Kettering's self-starter made it possible for more women to drive than ever before. When long skirts got tangled in milady's feet as she reached for the clutch pedal, then she made a basic alteration—shortened the hem of her skirt. Long tresses were whipped by the wind while driving; she bobbed her hair. The big hat then was relegated to the attic. Next she discarded her corset. The emancipation move gained momentum. Straight ahead was a long anticipated goal—women suffrage—and the automobile speeded up the process.

The glamour girl appeared more receptive to the charms of the boys with a car.

A.M.A.

When the low-priced family car began to haul commercial passengers, the cab business took a big spurt forward. This 1915 Ford sold for $690, fully equipped. Its modest price enabled numerous hack drivers to switch from horses to automobiles.
Black Star

CABS AND JITNEYS

With a car, a fellow could make a buck if he had to. By pausing at busy intersections, a driver readily picked up a carload of passengers, each willing to pay for the privilege of riding. During the sharp economic dip preceding World War I, many a car owner made a living by offering rides along well-traveled routes. The driver charged a nickel, the same as streetcars, but gave faster service.

The slang term for a five cent piece—"jitney"—soon was affixed to such vehicles. The term became legal terminology, when transit companies pressed for city ordinances to regulate this "unfair competition." Drivers who made a business of transporting people were known as "hackers" or "hackies" in the East. In the Midwest, they were generally called "cabbies."

Though special cab bodies were seen in a few Eastern cities, taxicab service in most communities grew out of the use of ordinary touring cars. Enterprising liverymen in rural communities offered motor service between towns to "drummers," summer visitors and other travelers. In larger cities, public hackers sensed the public preference for faster transportation than Dobbin offered, and many switched over to automobiles. Competition then forced taxicab rates below that of horse-drawn hacks, and more people began to patronize the motor cabs.

Intercity bus lines grew out of jitney service. Greyhound Lines, for example, began as a jitney bus line in Minnesota, when two enterprising young men in the iron range country used their Huppmobile touring car to carry iron miners to and from pits.

The 1915 jitney helped bring motorized public transportation service to the common man. For a nickel, he could ride across town as fast as the private motorist or the taxi-driven traveler. This popular form of transportation flourished until city transit lines began to provide motorbus service.
General Motors

R. E. Olds created a memorable impression by advertising his 1912 model as "My Farewell Car," which he insisted marked the ultimate in his, or anybody else's, manufacturing efforts.

Reo

TOM-TOM BEATERS

While cars were classed as novelties, the press hounded inventors for news. Once the product became commonplace, automobile men courted the newsmen. Nothing was too bombastic or fantastic to take to the press under the guise of news. No promotional stunt was too zany to attempt.

Henry Ford's publicity man, E. LeRoy Pelletier, once dispatched a story to the newspapers about his boss racing a thunderstorm across the city. According to the apocryphal yarn, Ford drove an open single-seater model the entire distance in bright sunshine, while the encroaching storm, at almost equal speed, pursued him. Occasionally, Ford had to slow down a bit to let his elemental adversary catch up. In a breathless finale, Ford raced into his garage, absolutely dry. But according to Pelletier, on inspecting the car's box body in the rear, Mr. Ford found it heaped high with enormous hailstones.

Another manufacturer with a publicity flare was Hugh Chalmers, who in 1910 put up Chalmers cars as first prize for the Major Leagues' champion batter. When the first American League award was won by his fellow townsman, Ty Cobb, the automobile manufacturer felt highly gratified. His ardor iced however, when Cobb immediately sold his Chalmers. The enraged manufacturer would have withdrawn the award if calmer heads had not prevailed. He consented to try it another year on a revised basis. A jury of baseball writers in 1911 were to determine the player of most value to his team. When the returns were in, again Ty Cobb had won!

Some forgotten phrase-coiner has applied the term "tom-tom beating" to the art of disseminating automotive news. With only a backward glance

HUSKY ROAD BLOCK
No obstacle in the road, even a human's prostrate form, would deter the Chalmers Six from its predetermined course, the manufacturer maintained. A local strong man provided the durable thighs, while the New York distributor furnished a couple of rugged 1914 models for the publicity stunt.

A.M.A.

at primitive Congo tribes who communicate with native drums, the American automotive practitioners used every means of attention-getting known to man. On occasions, they would employ monkeys, midgets, chorus beauties, or a member of royalty to attract attention to their products. Most publicity men placed their performers behind the steering wheel, though Chalmers did not hesitate to put his under the car.

When the press showed restraint in telling about his product's virtues, the manufacturer took paid space to tell the world himself. Splashy, self-praising advertisements became a pronounced feature in automobile merchandising. Not infrequently, some motor manufacturer would proclaim that he had achieved the ultimate in transportation. In eulogizing his 1912 Reo, R. E. Olds flatly said, "I do not believe that a car materially better will ever be built."

GEORGIA PEACH'S PRIZE
Ty Cobb, hero of Detroit, with his new Chalmers car that he won for leading the American League in batting in 1910.

A.M.A.

The closed car became elegant as well as comfortable.

A.M.A.

WINTER SHIVERS

At best, winter driving constituted a hazardous practice. Motorists venturing out in the snow took along their own shovels to clear the path. Even so, getting stuck was usually expected.

Only a few cars were closed; scant protection from the wind was afforded motorists by most models. Fabric or cape tops, known as one-man tops, appeared on the market in 1909, but side curtains didn't appear until nearly a decade later. Chains for tires helped provide traction on icy surfaces, if the owner was artful enough to get them on his tires.

The prevailing winter practice was to place jacks under all four wheels and leave the car in the woodshed until spring. But a growing number of motorists, from necessity or perversity, insisted on driving in winter.

The high wheels on this Model-T Ford scarcely were high enough to get through the drifted snow. Scene is Sandy Springs, Maryland. The date is 1914.

U.S. Bureau of Public Roads

LINCOLN HIGHWAYMEN

Big impetus to the good roads movement came through the Lincoln Highway Association, formed in 1912 to push road construction on the famed East-West route. Automobile and tire men provided leadership and cash, while communities along the way furnished manpower to construct "seedling miles" of highway. The marked increase in trade enjoyed by the pioneering towns, in turn, encouraged other communities to get busy. Caravans of cars made the trip over the Lincoln Highway in 1914 to publicize the progress.

The good roads movement quickly spread across the nation. Federal funds were first used in 1916 to develop rural post roads, and in 1919 the Federal Government paid out nearly three million dollars to states to help pay the cost of their state systems. In 1919, Oregon passed the first gasoline tax, which permitted further highway construction. Others quickly followed. All states had set up highway departments by 1919. Two years later, Congress passed the Federal Highways Act, which matched state expenditures dollar for dollar in the building of certain types of highway. The centuries of deplorable roads in America soon were to fade like yesterday's bad dream.

The American urge to "get away from it all" found a ready ally in the "tin lizzie." This low-cost mechanism for escape encouraged thousands of families to venture out into the great beyond.

So numerous did the tourists become that they formed organizations for mutual advice, help and information. The Tin Can Tourists' Association even adopted an emblem—a tin can tied to the car radiator cap—so that their comradeship could be widely recognized and extended. When meeting a fellow member, the tourist would seek his advice on the road ahead, where to find a camp site, how to repair a broken part. In turn, he would sketch a map on the road he'd come over, pointing out the detours, the muddy terrain or the domain of pestiferous constables.

TIN CAN TOURISTS

Main Street's monotony is relieved for Sinclair Lewis, who like any other Babbitt could jump in the tin Lizzie and rattle away to the wide-open spaces. The author and the first Mrs. Lewis are shown here in a 1913 Model T. Roadside picnics became an American institution, right, families could enjoy more privacy than in a restaurant, more freedom than in a city park, and less noise than staying home.

Theodore Roosevelt, hurrying as usual, is driving a Haynes car, while son Kermit sits stiffly in rear seat.

Brown Bros.

An age of outdoor recreation was dawning. No one had yet coined a "See America First" slogan, but it was being developed in practice. National parks felt the pick-up in business. Hunting and swimming activities increased. And golf began bursting out of its narrow bounds to become a mass sport: in 1914, the nation could count only 200 golf courses; in 1940, there were more than 5,000.

STAR PERFORMERS

The rich and famous, as well as the humble, found vacationing by automobile a treat. One summer Henry Ford, Thomas Edison, John Burroughs and Harvey Firestone went on a camping trip together. When the excursion was stalled because of a broken car fan, Ford himself repaired it. As the adjoining picture shows, the eminent quartette and their friends enjoyed various tastes as to wearing apparel on the camping trip. But they shared a mutual interest in mechanical objects like logging engines and mill wheels. Over the campfire, they discussed poetry, French fiction and patent law. While expressing a desire to rough it, they sometimes were tempted to accept the solid comforts of hotels and inns.

The phrenetic quality of Theodore Roosevelt in action is typified by the adjoining picture, showing him racing across the city by automobile.

FAMOUS VACATIONISTS
Ford, Firestone, Edison and Burroughs in 1918 took their vacation together. Like any four cronies who could afford it, they went by car. In fact, they took four cars and two supply trucks. Edison and Burroughs thought they should camp out every night, but the group compromised and stayed in hotels frequently. The above picture, taken at Green Island, shows from left to right: Harvey S. Firestone, Jr., Harvey, Sr., Thomas A. Edison, John Burroughs, Mayor James R. Watt of Albany, Henry Ford, Chauncey O. Haken and Samuel Ott.

Keystone View Co.

SLOW DEVELOPMENT

Though the Army experimented with motor vehicles back in 1899, the service's procurement policies lagged far behind. The mule was firmly imbedded in Army transport thinking, and the Quartermaster Department viewed motor transportation with skepticism. In early tests, vehicles for military usage ran only 25 miles before breaking down. The car above is a 1900 Davidson steam car, carrying a small gun and thin armor plate.

Robert J. Ickes Collection

A KICK AT THE ARMY MULE

The automobile had been kicking the carriage horse around for years when the motor truck took after the mule, mainstay of the Army. For its field transportation, the Army depended entirely on mules and wagons. Only a dozen motor trucks had been purchased by the Quartermaster Department, and they replaced horse-drawn drays at depots. Not until 1911 did the Army draw up specifications for a type of motor truck to replace the wagon in the field. At that time trucks were designed to operate on hard surfaces only. As the Army demanded that the vehicle must move wherever troops marched, few manufacturers sought the business.

Though it had never before built a truck, a small manufacturer in Clintonville, Wisconsin, became interested. The Four Wheel Drive Company, newly organized, had devised a method of applying power to all four wheels instead of just to the rear wheels. The Depot Quartermaster purchased the FWD vehicle, still equipped with passenger car chassis, for $1,904, and refitted it with a body similar to that used on Army escort wagons.

In 1916 General Pershing was sent into Mexico to track down Pancho Villa. Finding wagons too slow to supply his flying columns, Pershing demanded trucks. The Quartermaster Department scrambled to purchase any kind of truck, regardless of its suitability.

These soldiers could look at the oncoming Chalmers with academic interest, as the Army did not possess enough cars to take a single company for a ride at one time.

A.M.A.

Some 4,000 motor cars and trucks were picked up wherever they could be found. Manned with inexperienced drivers, inadequately equipped with spare parts, the trucks went forward when the order was given. Moving 200 miles into the Mexico desert, the motor caravan left in its wake cars and trucks broken down completely or suffering from bent frames, burned out engines and faulty ignition systems. When the hunt for Villa ended, and the troops returned to the border, fully two thousand motor vehicles were out of commission or left abandoned in the mud.

"But we had gained in experience," one writer reported three years later. "We had learned that the motor truck was a superior form of transport; and we had learned the need for special organization to make it serviceable."

MOTORS AT WAR

The automobile industry entered the period of the First World War a precocious adolescent. When the war was "over, over there," the industry had become a full-grown, powerful giant in the world economy.

Production figures: it took the industry from 1900 to 1914 to reach an annual output of a half million cars a year. But in 1915, under the stimulus of booming times, the industry produced 895,000 cars. The following year, the output exceeded 1,500,000. Cars were really selling! Super-salesman Hugh Chalmers in a forty minute harangue before 600 Chalmers dealers disposed of his entire 1916 schedule of 13,000 cars.

When America entered the war in April, 1917, cars continued to sell, despite the drafting of millions of young men, who were the best potential buyers of light cars.

Autos, autos, autos. They were everywhere—at recruiting drives, at war bond rallies, in parades, outside factories and hospitals, and increasing, on the road on Sunday afternoon. And often the driver was a woman.

Women workers took over jobs vacated by enlisting men. Soon they were making motors and tires, acting as conductors on streetcars and driving taxis. Expert women drivers formed ambulance corps. When the 1918 flu epidemic struck, patients were rushed from home to hospital in cars driven by women.

The women rushed to the aid of their country, forming motor corps, serving as mechanics, and acting as ambulance drivers.

Frederic Lewis

Traffic jam in French town near the Somme front.

Breakdown of rail transportation gave stimulus to long distance hauling by truck. President Wilson appointed Roy D. Chapin chief of the Highway Transport Commission. Chapin had Army trucks driven from factory to the seaboard rather than use rail flat cars. Some 30,000 trucks destined for France were loaded with war supplies and sent Eastward over bad roads. They detoured around unsafe bridges, wallowed in mud and clay, but managed to get through to the seaports.

Civilian production of motor trucks had never exceeded 25,000 a year prior to 1914. Encouraged with priorities, and hailed as being essential to the war program, civilian truck production in 1918 streaked upward to a 227,250 unit production figure.

The automobile made a dramatic stage entrance into modern warfare when General Gallieni mobilized Paris taxicabs to rush troops to the Marne in the summer of 1914 to stem the German offensive. A quarter of a million motor vehicles ultimately experienced service in France. Before the United States became involved in the conflict, such automobile manufacturers as Mack, White, Pierce-Arrow, Diamond T, Four Wheel Drive, Packard and others were making trucks for the Allies. After America declared war in April, 1917, virtually all the car manufacturers supplied motor vehicles— passenger cars for officers' use, ambulances on passenger car chassis, and a growing number of special service trucks.

General Pershing arrives at the Elysée Palace to pay his respects to the French president, who had sent his car around, a motor victoria.
Keystone View Co.

Lord Curzon observed that the outcome of the conflict was a "victory of Allied motors over German railroads." At Verdun, when railroads were rendered ineffectual, the French had to transport all their men and supplies over one thirty-four mile long road, reaching back to Bar-le-Duc. In the great Somme defense and in the brilliant victory drive, motor vehicles added an important element to the Allied cause.

Motor vehicles were used to carry aid to the sick and wounded at the front, and to bring relief to the needy in war-devastated areas. Folks back home contributed ambulances and relief trucks to the Red Cross for. alleviating the war suffering. As a messenger of mercy, the American motor vehicle became a welcome sight in France and Belgium.

Great jubilance greeted the end of the war on November 11, 1918. Factory sirens sounded. Automobiles sped up and down the streets, their horns blowing. The downtown sections were crowded with cars moving in a paper blizzard. At an end were the anxious months of worrying about the boys overseas. Gone, too, was sugar rationing, and the gas-less Sundays, when to venture out in a "pleasure car" was to be hailed "Slacker." It was time for celebration, for parades, for homecomings.

The war produced countless changes, for better or worse. Many Americans gained their first experience with motor vehicles in the Army. Training courses in automotive mechanics developed a large group of men whose skills were applied in peacetime as automotive engineers, mechanics and garage men. Others, learning how to handle trucks, entered inter-city truck business following the Armistice.

World War I changed, too, the Army's concept of transportation. Trucks became an inegral part of their supply chains, vanquishing the horse and mule except for a few specialized tasks.

Indianapolis staged its Victory parade in late 1918.

W. H. Bass Photo Co.

Brown Bros.

ALWAYS FAIR WEATHER
The silk-shirt era was at an end; the postwar boom had not yet begun. But the automobile was fast becoming a necessity, or in academic language, "a means of escape from the monotony of our day-by-day surroundings." One fair day in 1919 the relaxed group, above, sought relaxation at the Danbury Fair.

Chapter 3

FOUR WHEELS, NO BRAKES (1919-1929)

BOOM, BOOM

WITH the war ended, people could buy the things they really wanted. The pent-up yearning to venture beyond the horizon stirred the people. The typical American family wanted a car. By hook or by crook, it got a car.

At the beginning of 1919, America had six million automobiles. Four years later the number had doubled. And a decade after the war ended, the number had grown to twenty-three million.

"You might say that 1919 was the year before the deluge," transportation historian Franklin M. Reck observed. "It was in 1919 that people finally decided, once and for all, that automobiling was more than a recreation. It was a necessity."

Automobile travel was becoming, too, an all-year-round, day-and-night proposition. People could motor in relative comfort. They were getting self-starters and electric lights. Demountable rims made tire-changing easier. And they began to demand—and get—closed cars. In 1919, nine out of ten cars were open models. A decade later, the ratio was reversed: 90 per cent were closed models.

"You might say that 1919 marked the beginning of the modern automobile age," Mr. Reck contended, and went on to say:

> It marked the beginning of the greatest car-and-highway building age the world has ever seen.
>
> There is always a simple explanation for a miracle like this. The automobile eame along and gave us something we had never completely possessed before. It gave us a sense of freedom, a feeling of independence, an escape from the monotony of our day-by-day surroundings.

More cars were built in a single year, 1923, than had been constructed from the birth of the industry through the end of 1915.

In 1923, more than thirteen million passenger cars were in use in the United States. Four states—New York, Pennsylvania, New Jersey and Maryland—had more cars in service than the entire world outside the United States. (And a not-to-be-proud-of note: More cars are *stolen* annually in a group of twenty-eight American cities than are used in Austria, Belgium, Japan or Mexico.)

Thousands of city dwellers flocked to the shore on week ends in their cars. Getting home on a Sunday evening, especially for those who depended on ferryboats to cross back into the city, was another matter.

Motorists, below, waiting in line for ferry to Jersey in 1920. Two years later work was begun on the Holland Tunnel.

TRAFFIC JAM

The National Geographic predicted that the saturation point in car demand would not be an economic condition, but rather a physical one. "The congestion in big cities is fast growing so great as to keep thousands of motorists out of downtown districts," it reported in October, 1923.

In Manhattan, every twenty-four hours some 42,000 motor vehicles were passing the corner at Fifth Avenue at Forty-second Street; 4,500 an hour were not unusual. The Fifth Avenue block-signal system, controlled by a central tower, "has accomplished much, but even it is destined to become inadequate," *The National Geographic* writer predicted. But Chicago apparently was in worse shape.

"So great is the congestion in the famous Loop District in Chicago that proposals are being made to take all pedestrians off the street level and provide second story sidewalks for them," he reported.

Some of the pleasure began to be drained out of "pleasure car" riding. Sunday, particularly, was trying. Pleasure parks, picnic groves and bathing beaches were jammed with cars. Along the Jersey shore on a Sunday evening, motorists were lined up bumper to bumper for mile after mile, waiting their turn on the ferries to Manhattan. Exhausted, bedraggled, bleary-eyed families frequently were still sitting in their cars at midnight, after a seven hour wait for a chance at the ferry. One ray of hope was offered these hapless motorists: on October 26, 1922, work was begun on a tunnel under the Hudson River between Jersey City and Manhattan.

Traffic congestion didn't stop with the big metropolis. Cities and towns, too, suddenly realized they'd have to provide stop lights, stop streets, traffic rules and many other things they hadn't given much thought to

Detroit's first traffic light consisted of a railroad switch lantern borrowed from the Michigan Central Railroad. This oil-fed device gave way to another type charged with storage batteries. It had a handle which the traffic officer could turn. Not until 1921 did the Motor City attempt to synchronize traffic lights at two intersections, where heretofore a police officer turned a switch manually which changed the lights.

Detroit installed crows' nests at busy intersections. A police officer manned each tower-like structure and manually operated a semaphore labeled with "Stop and Go." This photograph, right, taken in 1921, on Fifth Avenue near 51st Street, indicates degree of traffic. To try to control its growing congestion, New York installed a central tower on Fifth Avenue in the early twenties. With 4,500 motor vehicles using the street in one hour, it soon became inadequate.

Ewing Galloway

HAND-ME-DOWN
To move new cars, the dealers had to accept trade-ins. Average resale price of these cars was estimated at $308. In 1922 there were three trade-ins to five new-car sales.

THE WHEELS KEEP TURNING

Who can afford a car? One automobile industry veteran grunted an observation:

"It's just like a question of whether a man can afford to get married or not."

To make it easier for the prospect to decide that the answer should be "Yes," finance companies stepped up their deferred payment plans. Installment buying dates from 1915, but relatively few financiers paid much attention to it, until the booming twenties got under way. By 1923, seven out of ten cars were sold "on time." The usual basis was about one-third down with the balance in twelve equal payments.

Ford offered a "five dollars down and five a week" scheme. His dealers promptly enrolled hundreds of thousands of new customers.

Many families also began to shop around for a good used car. These second-hand vehicles usually had many useful miles of transportation in them, and they were priced considerably under a new model. The average allowance given to a new customer on his trade-in was $322, according to the National Automobile Dealers Association. But the dealer resold the used car for about $308, they figured. Factories kept the process lively by restyling their makes yearly in an effort to make their customers dissatisfied with what they had. Five years after the war, the American public was spending $3,000,000,000 on new cars and another $1,000,000,000 on used cars.

Economists put in a plug, terming the motor car "a definite element in our standard of living." The president of Baldwin Locomotive Works told his men he wanted them to have initiative enough to own cars.

Car sales reached five million in 1923, if one included nearly a million and a half used cars that changed hands. One writer commented, "This means that one family out of every four in the country annually figures in an automobile transaction."

Car registrations had reached a point where they were only a million behind the telephone listings in the nation, only seven million behind the total number of dwellings. In an era of superlatives, the automobile was Big Time business.

FETCHED FROM THE FARM

The song writers could well inquire, "How are you going to keep them down on the farm?" The city's bright lights and easy dollars attracted the young folks. The motor industries of Detroit, Flint, Toledo and South Bend contributed their share of allurement.

With European immigration shut off during the war, the automotive industry had recruited workers from all over the nation. They flocked in from Midwest farms. They left depressed mining areas. They crossed the border from Canada. And they even slipped out of the kitchen to the factory.

In the first postwar year, 1919, nearly 30,000 women were working in auto plants, or about five times as many as before the war. However, single young men made up the bulk of the recruits.

Wages were good as new building boomed. But even if a man didn't have the cash for a new car, he could buy "on time." Seven out of ten cars were sold on the installment plan in 1923.

A.M.A.

By the time Willys produced its millionth car, the "boys" in the factory had made up with president John N. Willys.

Wages averaged around $25 a week, which looked good to the farm hand. But to the farmer, these wage rates appeared a sinister plot.

From Governor A. E. Sleeper of Michigan came a ripsnorting blast. Automobile makers are "seducing" the lads and girls from Michigan farms, he charged. In Detroit, they'd only lead lives of extravagance and spend their money foolishly, while the farms went to rack and ruin. He warned that "Michigan will wake up hungry unless some of Michigan's manhood is left to run its farms."

Returning service men came into car factories in big numbers. Some 35,000 automobile factory workmen and mechanics had been drafted during the war, according to General Crowder of Selective Service. Several thousand were placed in Detroit in a few weeks' time in early 1919. Of the total number registered, 78 per cent got jobs. An unknown number didn't bother with the placement office, but got their own jobs.

In 1919, according to the Census of Manufactures, some 396,000 people were working in automobile, body and parts plants. That was 271 per cent more than in 1914.

The industry's transition to peacetime production was smooth and labor friction was low. One exception was a long strike at the Willys Company, then one of the largest manufacturers in the industry. It employed 14,000 workers at Toledo and elsewhere. In March, 1919, organized workers, led by the machinists, proposed an increase in wages and a reduction in hours of work. The company countered with an announcement of a profits distribution plan, a company union and an increase in hours of work. When the union men refused to work more than eight hours daily, a combination strike-lockout developed in Toledo, which was not settled until early 1920.

Willys' profit sharing was one of many plans launched in the postwar period. General Motors established employee savings systems for stock purchase. The Apperson Company gave its workers 25 per cent of its profits. Studebaker adopted a broad program of profit-sharing, free vacations, disability pensions, and housing in order to promote stability of employment.

TRUCKS GET GOING

When the war ended, the future didn't look too promising for industry's ugly duckling, the motor truck.

The War Department had on hand more military trucks than it could use. This surplus hung like a pall over the domestic market; manufacturers feared that if the government unloaded this surplus on the public, the supply would put a decided crimp in their business. Moreover, the nation's deplorable roadbeds hindered truck operations. Shippers placed little reliance in trucks meeting schedules. Compared to other forms of transportation, the truck looked like a luxury.

Roger Babson, the economic seer, in 1921 confided to his clients:

"We are not bullish on tractors and trucks. With farm horses selling at $25 to $50. . . .we see no reason for a much greater sale of tractors and trucks."

But the future didn't prove as gloomy as predicted.

By a happy chain of circumstances, the government surplus turned out to be a blessing. The Post Office Department took 6,000 of the vehicles, equipped them with screen bodies, and put them to work hauling mail. The Public Health Service received 780 trucks for use in constructing veterans' hospitals. Most important, however, was the disposal of 28,000 trucks to the Bureau of Public Roads. This agency distributed them to the state highway departments. They were put promptly to work building roads. Big trucks were fitted out with dump bodies, hoisting devices and other special equipment for hauling gravel and stone. Ambulances were converted into portable offices. Other vehicles, ingeniously transformed, were used for sprinkling and snow clearance. This equipment proved as useful as money to the states, and gave tremendous impetus to the nation's badly needed highway construction program.

STORE AT THE DOOR
The traveling grocery store developed in the twenties. Many a community not on a railroad began to get daily deliveries of merchandise from the city by truck. A reverse flow found the farmer hauling his produce direct to the city housewife, thus eliminating the middleman and giving the city customer freshly picked fruits and vegetables.

A.M.A.

An early version of the Bookmobile was this 1926 vehicle used by the Evanston, Illinois, public library to take reading material to children in new neighborhoods.

A critical shortage of railroad shipping space in the spring of 1920 resulted in a priority system on freight movement. Automobile manufacturers discovered that Washington held a low appraisal of the essential need for its passenger product. Refused freight cars, the manufacturers turned to trucks for getting raw materials to their production lines.

All over America people found ways to use trucks. In 1922, two Vermont boys, Harry and Mickey Zabarsky, bought a truck to haul groceries from Boston to towns in northeastern Vermont. In Chicago, an ice and coal dealer contracted to carry a cargo of merchandise by truck all the way to Milwaukee. A jobless veteran in Virginia, planked down his $500 bonus for a secondhand truck, and rolled out on the highway looking for something to do. A Grand Rapids drayman, bought several trucks to augment his horse-and-wagon fleet and ventured to nearby cities with loads of goods. (Today his "Interstate Motor Freight System" serves sixteen states, employs 1500 people, keeps 500 trucks busy daily).

Shippers took a dim view of trucks and their ability to get the goods delivered when needed. In view of the state of the roads, this was hardly an unreasonable attitude. Yet, pioneers like the Zabarskys managed to get their merchandise through despite hell and, frequently, high water. Mickey drove through floods while Harry sat on a front fender holding a long pole, plumbing water holes to see if the truck could make it. They drove up mountain sides with a helper walking behind, ready to jam a rock under the rear wheel when the truck stalled. They got through so often, despite the conditions, that the shippers' faith mounted. Today the Zabarsky's St. Johnsbury Trucking Company serves 2,700 New England towns, and does $2,500,000 of business a year.

There were thousands more pioneers. And as the nation's highway program accelerated, and more than 3,000,000 miles of rural roads became surfaced, the trucks pressed close on the heels of the steam roller to offer countless new services.

Farmers took to trucking livestock to market. Cattle lost less weight in transit via motor carriers compared to railroad cars. The trucks' flexibility, too, meant the farmer could take advantage of higher prices prevailing at other stock yards. The produce farmer, by selling his fruits and vegetables off his truck, got a bigger share of the housewife's dollar. Some set up door-to-door routes in the city.

Newspaper trucks penetrated rural areas, eliminating the one-day delay in mail delivery of the news. In the city, newspaper trucks speeded through the streets with fresh editions, serving as spear carriers in circulation wars.

City libraries equipped trucks with special bodies and took books to young patrons in parks, playgrounds and new neighborhoods lacking branches. State libraries carried literature to remote areas which never had public facilities.

Performing these and countless other functions, the truck began to help transform the pattern of American lives, manners and habits.

Within three years after Mr. Babson's gloomy appraisal, more than a million new trucks had been sold. Three new trucks were being produced for every one manufactured in 1921.

Connecticut set up a weighing station in 1923 in connection with a transportation survey. Trucks already were becoming a heavy user of the highways.

O'Dell & Shields

HIGH STAKES

Turning into the southwest curve at the Indianapolis Speedway, these racers of recent date start their first lap of the 200-lap race. Indianapolis merchants donate $100 in prize money to the contestant leading the field at the end of each lap. Ralph DePalma in 1921 earned more than $10,000 in such prizes before being forced out by mechanical difficulties. Begun in 1911, the Indianapolis race immediately became a magnet for motorists from every state in the Union.

Brown Bros.

Ray Harroun, first winner of the Indianapolis race, introduced rear-view mirror. Tommy Milton poses in a Frontenac, right, following his 1921 victory. Behind him, cigar in evidence, is Barney Oldfield. To Barney's left is Louis Chevrolet.

SPEEDWAY

With the excitement of the war over, Americans again turned to automobile racing for thrills. At dawn on Memorial Day to 10:00 A.M., when the starting bomb exploded, 150,000 or more Americans swarmed through the gates of the Indianapolis Motor Speedway.

There were license plates from forty-eight states; campers arrived three and four days before the event, and on race day made a grand rush for the gates. Inside they staged fender fights to gain the best positions along the fence. Some cars carried their own grandstands, consisting of a trestle fitting over the car hood. On this were placed boards and cushions, where spectators could sit in elevated position to peer over other cars.

Outside the grounds, Indianapolis police handled the biggest traffic of the year. Motorcycle policemen constantly moved along the routes, shouting to drivers to "double up" and to "step on it."

The morning traffic, staggered over five or six hours, was orderly compared to the melee at the end of the race. With the race winner determined, virtually everyone in a car tried to leave the grounds at once. Hoosier residents wanted to get home by supper, out-state drivers tried to pile up miles before dark. A seemingly endless caravan of cars, in close

Highly popular racing figure of the early twenties was Jimmy Murphy, shown at Uniontown, Pennsylvania, just before a meet. Murphy won the 1922 race at Indianapolis. Right, the four winners at the Uniontown, Pennsylvania, races on June 19, 1920 all drove Duesenberg cars. In car No. 10, the driver was a virtual newcomer, Tommy Milton, who won first place and later became one of the nation's outstanding drivers; second place went to Jimmy Murphy, in car No. 12; third place was captured by Eddie O'Donnell in car No. 29; and fourth place went to I. J. Fetterman in car No. 31.

When stock cars needed testing, Cannonball Baker was usually there driving them. His endurance runs made headlines throughout the twenties.
Frederic Lewis

formation, moved snail-like on the National Road, leading east and west from "The Crossroads of America," as Hoosiers proudly proclaimed their capital. As years went by, and the speed of racing cars increased, the duration of the race diminished. The new arteries provided more ways to escape from the torrent of traffic. Nowadays, spectators get back to Chicago, Columbus, Louisville, the same evening of the race. But in 1920, motorists were lucky to get out of Marion County by nightfall.

Since 1911, the 500 mile race at Indianapolis had claimed the honor of being the nation's premier racing event. On May 30 that year, Ray Harroun, in a Marmon Wasp, averaged 74 m.p.h., to win. His car carried an unique device—a rear view mirror—first used on any car.

Idol of the racing fans was Ralph DePalma who came within five heart-breaking miles of winning the 1912 race. With victory a few minutes away, a broken piston put his Mercedes out of the race. As the crowd roared its encouragement, DePalma and Rupert Jeffkins, his mechanic, desperately shoved the car along the track. After pushing the heavy car two miles, DePalma reached his pits nearly exhausted. Joe Dawson, in a National, meanwhile had flashed over the finish line. DePalma's sportsmanship in the face of misfortune endeared him to the racing world, and he became a favorite wherever he raced.

First place was captured in ensuing races by French and German makes—Peugeot, Delage and Mercedes. Not until 1920 did an American car win another Indianapolis race. That year Gaston Chevrolet, driving an American-built Monroe, averaged 88.16 m.p.h. to nose out Rene Thomas in a French Ballot for first prize money. From now on, American racing machines kept their supremacy.

A youthful new star, Tommy Milton, now flashed into racing fame. Having won at Uniontown the previous year, he set his sights on the big race in Indianapolis in 1921. When a trial run convinced him that his

Frontenac's bearings were too tight, he and his mechanics started to work replacing thirty-two bearings. They did not complete the job until 2:00 A.M. the very day of the race. After catching a few hour's sleep, Milton climbed confidently into his car, kept a steady but safe pace and waited for his chance. It came on the 112th lap. Ralph DePalma, who had been keeping a heavy foot on the throttle of his Ballot, heard his engine stutter. DePalma found in the pits that the Ballot's bearings were gone and a connecting rod was broken. Taking over the lead, Milton gnawed casually on a red apple as he roared around the track. He ended up with $26,200 in lap moneys and first prize.

Milton's car, a Frontenac, was built by the racing star of earlier days, Louis Chevrolet, whose name had been bestowed on the Chevrolet passenger car. He was one of a select little group of racing car designers, who could clean up $50,000 or more a season if their cars showed up well at Indianapolis, Uniontown, Altoona and other tracks.

Another famous designer, Harry A. Miller, developed front-wheel drive cars, which became the sensation of gasoline alley. Even more successful were August and Fred Duesenberg, who produced cars regularly at their Indianapolis plant, and whose racing teams for years won about half of all races held in America. The Duesenbergs became the first passenger car builders to adopt the straight eight motor, the four wheel brake and the hydraulic brake. Jimmy Murphy, who placed fourth at the 1921 race in Indianapolis, had four wheel brakes on his Duesenberg. The following year, the popular Jimmy Murphy broke all existing records at Indianapolis to win first place. He averaged 94.4 m.p.h. in a car with a Duesenberg chassis and Miller engine.

Tommy Milton again took first place in 1923, becoming the first two-time winner. His mount was an H.C.S., the initials of auto maker Harry C. Stutz. Milton demonstrated once more his gumption. When his hands became so badly blistered that he could scarcely grip the steering wheel,

Duke Nalon, driving a Novi in the 1949 race, fortunately got out alive when his car caught fire.

Towers

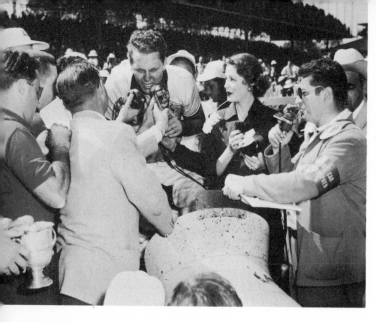

Winner of 1952 race was Troy Ruttman, who earned a smile from movie actress Arlene Dahl.
O'Dell & Shields

he momentarily left the race to get his hands bandaged. Then he resumed his grueling job until the checkered flag acclaimed him the winner at the 200th lap.

How does it feel to ride in a racer? A writer named Homer McKee in 1922 felt he knew. He expressed it as follows:

> Did you ever ride ninety miles an hour in an open race car no bigger than a bathtub, with the sun frying your brain, wind crushing you against the back of your seat, ears splitting with the crash of cylinders —the track and the world and your past pulling back under you like a torrent of milk, and all the while the blinding glimmer of the stretch ahead— always AHEAD—rising up to slam you in the face?
>
> It's HELL, but a kind of happy hell that hairy men come back to year after year.

Racing fans heard a disconcerting bit of news at the end of the 1923 race. Carl G. Fisher, founder and president, publicly debated whether or not to continue the Speedway. He'd built the plant for scientific work; the sporting interest was secondary as far as he was concerned and would be in the future, he stated. Therefore, he was calling car manufacturers and others together to decide whether they really wanted the big practical testing laboratory.

Fisher soon relinquished the Speedway control. His partner, James G. Allison became president. Later one-time racing star, Eddie Rickenbacker, headed a group that bought the big racing plant; and still later another ex-driver, Wilbur Shaw, became president. The Indianapolis Motor Speedway's chief use was for staging a sporting event of international interest annually on Memorial Day.

The automobile makers mostly relied on their own engineering and testing facilities for car development. To publicize their makes, they engaged such colorful figures as Cannonball Baker and Barney Oldfield to stage cross-country endurance runs. As for the high-speed contests, they largely left that field to the specialty designers and their drivers. However, the Speedway continued to be a laboratory for testing of automotive parts, ranging from piston rings to spark plugs.

One significant contribution to the aircraft industry can be traced to the track. Between races, Jim Allison kept racing teams employed in engine development. Basic ideas were worked out there for the Allison engine, which was to figure so prominently in World War II aerial combat. And from the Indianapolis Speedway shops evolved a superior type engine bearing, now widely used in aircraft.

Activity around the pits always fascinates the spectators.
Towers Photographers

BATTLE'S END
Woodrow Wilson, his great dream of America's participation in the League of Nations blasted by an obdurate Senate, leaves the White House for his home on "S" street, as well-wishers bid him farewell.
Harris & Ewing

HEADLINERS

His health wrecked over the League of Nations battle, Woodrow Wilson is seen above riding away from the White House in 1921. A lame, disillusioned man, he lived three more years in his house on "S" Street, went for occasional motor trips around Washington.

His successor, the amiable Warren G. Harding, was the first Chief Executive to use an automobile to ride in the inaugural parade. He also was the first president who could drive. President Harding in the accompanying picture is shown leaving for the Capitol in 1922 to present the Four Power Pacific Treaty to the Senate for ratification.

Calvin Coolidge, as Governor of Massachusetts, won national attention by calling out the entire State Guard to settle a Boston police strike. He told labor leader Samuel Gompers: "There is no right to strike against the public safety, by anybody, anywhere, any time." His friends started a move to get him into the White House, settled for the vice-presidential nomination. Two years later he succeeded to the presidency when Harding died. In his term of office, Congress removed the war-imposed luxury tax on automobiles.

President Harding leaves the White House for the Senate, which awaited his message on the Four Power treaty. Calvin Coolidge, a tight-lipped Yankee, kept his public manners as restrained as his car and his clothes. He is shown in 1921, at right, the year he was elected vice-president.

Keystone

Harris & Ewin

Colorful campaigner Al Smith conveys warm greetings to tenants of Manhattan's skyscrapers.

Al Smith, who rose from an Oliver Street fish wagon to four terms as Governor of New York, captivated the people wherever he went in Manhattan. On riding down Fifth Avenue, Smith and his brown derby provided a lovable target for ticker tape. Gaining the Democratic nomination for president in 1928, he boldly declared that the 18th Amendment must be amended.

His Republican opponent, Herbert Hoover, hitched his wagon to the star of prosperity. He said: "Given a chance to go forward with the policies of the last eight years, we shall soon, with the help of God, be in the sight of the day when poverty will be banished from this nation." He won the election, and soon began to struggle with the problems of a receding national economy.

Queen Marie of Roumania staged a triumphal tour of America in 1927, gained capital loans for her Balkan country. Manhattan's official greeter, Grover Whalen, donned his silk hat, met her boat at Quarantine, then whisked her off to City Hall in a Packard. Edward Prince of Wales, dream prince of the twenties, also visited the United States. Packards provided him transportation.

Babe Ruth receives some tangible tokens of his fans' affection — a dog and a car. Coach Knute Rockne, right, trainer of championship Notre Dame football teams, had his name conferred on a car — The Rockne Six.

Studebaker president A. R. Erskine ropes humorist Will Rogers in a playful moment in 1925, a period when the South Bend company was getting a noose around a sizable share of the automotive market.
Studebaker Corp.

Acclaim that exceeded even that accorded royalty was reserved for Babe Ruth, the "Sultan of Swat." The home run king of the New York Yankees is shown in Detroit, where admirers gave him a new car and a Great Dane dog. The other players are Detroit stars Harry Heilmann and Ty Cobb.

Rudolph Valentino, who catapulted to stardom after his first movie *The Four Horsemen of the Apocalypse,* lived in a lavish style befitting his income. His hilltop den, Falcon's Lair, featured black painted interior walls and mourning-draped windows. For the open road, however, he favored milky-white Italian roadsters. He died heavily in debt in 1926.

Dark, handsome, romantic Rudolph Valentino lavished his film fortune on somber interiors and flashy exteriors. The Original Our Gang Kids, right, whose antics tickled the funnybone of millions of movie-goers, pose with props provided by Studebaker.

Brown Bros.   *Studebaker C*

GYPSY CORPUSCLES
These female tourists are shown
11,306 feet above sea level at
Empire Cone, Berthond Pass,
outside Denver.
Denver Tourist Bureau

SUMMER NOMADS

"If you have a car, any make, any year, anything that will run, you
have all you need for a vacation," advised George W. Sutton, Jr., in
Collier's in 1921. "A million Americans have found this out."

A great urge came over Americans to see the West—that romantic,
remote, formerly inaccessible region beyond the corn belt. The tourists
found a hearty welcome. Almost every town on the main routes provided
camping sites that were "as unfailing as the Post Office and the Public
Library."

These "motor campers," lugging their own tents, refrigerator baskets,
gasoline cans and other paraphernalia, swarmed over the national parks.
In the summer of 1920, 35,000 had camped out in Yellowstone; another
25,000 at Yosemite. Denver boasted 800 camp lots within its city limits,

Nearly 1,500,000 persons visited
the national parks in 1924, three
times as many as in 1917. One
writer commented: "Gypsy corpuscles in the blood of the nation were suddenly released by
the general family ownership of
the means of independent, un-
hampered, long-distance travel."
Shown above are motorists waiting to get into Yellowstone National Park on opening day in
June, 1923.
J. E. Haynes

Niagara Falls stood out as a top attraction for sight-seeing Americans in the East. The automobile replaced the excursion train as the chief transportation medium for reaching the Falls.

piped water free to thirsty motorists. Santa Barbara did it up deluxe style. Hanging up a sign, "Cleanliness is Our Joy and Pride," the coastal city offered campers use of waffle irons, electric washing machines, curling irons and nail files.

For the dudes, one fashion writer recommended the following men's wearing apparel: snugly-fitting knickerbockers, puttees, wrap leggings or canvas leggings, two suits of light wool underwear, one cap for driving, and buckskin driving gloves with ventilated backs. But the typical masculine traveler was apt to be wearing the Hart, Schaffner & Marx suit that he wore to Rotary.

"I hereby elect motor camping the most democratic sport in America," a writer for *Outlook* exulted.

Homebodies, who knew Colorado, Wyoming and Utah only as large blocks on colored maps, got off their verandas to learn geography at first-hand. They kept detailed records and trotted out their expense sheets to anyone interested to prove that it was cheaper to travel than to stay at home.

"It is quite a good thing to look at this world now and then with bare eyes," exclaimed a tourist of the twenties.

Keystone View

TENTING ON THE NEW CAMP GROUND
Yosemite National Park's scenery provided a magnet that attracted motorists from all over the nation. California realized $10,000,000 in tourist expenditures in 1924 as a result of Yosemite's lure alone, travel authorities estimated.
U.S. Dept. of Interior

Harper's pundit, Edward S. Martin, writing from the vantage point of "The Editor's Easy Chair" gave testimony:

> It is cheaper to live in a Ford than in a house . . . Living in a Ford is like having creation brought to you on a plate . . . It makes one realize why, when motor cars were first being disseminated, one read of so many people mortgaging their houses to buy them.

In a jovial sell-out of his own craft, Martin concluded:

> One great relief we got from the Ford was the lapse of all obligation to read anything . . . To read all the time is like seeing life through somebody else's spectacles. It is quite a good thing to look at this world now and then with bare eyes.

The West, alive to the possibilities of tourist trade, pioneered in providing motor camps, information booths, travel bureaus and other services for motorists. An estimated 1,000 camps were spread throughout the West, and 200 in California alone. "The idea is spreading Eastward," one writer observed, "and has reached Springfield, Massachusetts."

Thriving from the out-of-state trade, resort people hailed their scenery as "the new cash crop." Florida authorities in 1925 estimated that tourists from other states spent $1,000,000,000 in one season enjoying its scenery. Minnesota entertained 150,000 tourists from other states, the majority of

The camp grounds swarmed with tourists at the dedication of Wind River Road in Twogwotee Pass at Yellowstone Park. The tepees in the foreground were headquarters of Shoshone and Arapaho Indian Chiefs.

National Park Service

whom camped out. California claimed tourists expenditures amounted to $500,000,000 a year.

A weather-beaten Vermont farmer confided to a magazine writer:

> From now on, tourists are goin' to be my meat. I've changed my mind about scenery. It's the greatest crop these hills have ever raised.

In the late summer of 1923 Vermont's tourist trade received a stimulation of avalanche proportions. In the morning of August 3, newspaper readers learned that in an old-fashioned farmhouse at Plymouth, Vermont, taciturn Calvin Coolidge had stood before a kerosene lamp, placed his hand on the family Bible, and repeated after his father:

"I do solemnly swear that I will faithfully execute the office of President of the United States. . ."

Vacationers, looking up this remote spot on the map, detoured miles to drive by the farmhouse and its nearby landmark, the "Notch." Sensing what was happening, John Garibaldi, an old friend of Coolidge's, rented all available space on the "Notch" not occupied by buildings, to keep the post card hawkers, peanut vendors and soft drink dispensers from ruining the scenery with stands and painted signs. He then badgered the Vermont legislature into providing funds to improve the roads in the area. His foresight was fully justified. The following summer Coolidge returned to the Plymouth farm for his vacation. Some famous tourists, among them Ford, Edison and Firestone, dropped by for a visit. Hordes of other motorists streamed through town all summer long. Some 60,000 automobiles, carrying 270,000 people, descended on Plymouth that year.

Tourists' travel was swelling steadily throughout the nation. By 1925, Americans claimed six times as many passenger cars as all the rest of the world. The slogan, "See America First" became a national chorus as 15,000,000 Americans turned gypsy every summer.

Among the well-known nomads of the day was H. S. Firestone (right), the tire king, who had a special truck equipped for touring.

BODY ASSEMBLY
Workmen pushed cars from one station to the next before the moving assembly line became standard in production procedures. Lowering the car body onto the chassis required time and considerable patience.

CHANGING TECHNOLOGY

Staggering though it was, production in the twenties at times lagged behind the seemingly insatiable demand for cars. One bottleneck blocking greater production was body building. Many a sales chief, back from a trip with invoices for carloads of new automobiles, turned livid on being informed that the production department hadn't yet caught up with previous orders.

Iron-fisted production man, Charles Sorenson, on being needled by Ford's sales manager to get busy on his backlog, snapped: "If I ever do catch up with you, you're through."

By painting his cars black and never varying the hue, Ford partially minimized a great headache. Those manufacturers who catered to the public's taste for color, however, had a big storage problem on their hands. It took about seventeen days to put the finish on a low-priced car. More expensive models required thirty days. If dirt blew through an open window onto the varnish, it meant starting all over again.

As many as twenty coats of slow-drying oil paints and varnishes had to be applied by brush. Rejects sometimes ran as high as 20 per cent of total output. Twenty million dollars might be tied up in 15,000 unfinished cars during a heavy production schedule. To find space, production managers utilized everything but the gent's room vestibule.

Paint and automotive technicians undertook joint research to try to solve the problem. Their starting point was cellulose nitrate, a chemical used in making wartime explosives. It proved dangerous to use and re-

Building car bodies in the twenties was slow and tedious work.

sulted in some serious factory fires and explosions. After hitting upon less dangerous coatings, they settled on a fast drying, spray lacquer. That did the trick. Used first in 1924 on the Oakland, the new method promptly swept the industry. It reduced the time required to finish an automobile body from days to hours. With today's infra-red lights and reflectors, drying time has been further reduced to six hours.

One problem solved, a dozen more appeared. In 1924 Chrysler brought out an "all-steel" body. Competitors, quick to note their rattle, dubbed them "tin cans." Anxious hours were spent in engineering laboratories developing sound deadeners and noise-absorbing materials to eliminate the nuisance.

Steel rusting presented another headache. Then technicians unearthed another wartime product: the rust preventatives used on mines in the North Sea. They provided a splendid undercoat for car bodies.

Much more difficult, however, was the task of building the body in the first place. All-metal bodies required sheet steel in wide strips, capable of taking deep draws in the presses. A quest for making wide sheets of steel by continuous rolling methods had been going on since 1904. Finally John Titus Butler, using war-surplus machinery in an experiment in Ashland, Kentucky, achieved partial success in 1923. The problem of subjecting sheet steel to deep drawing presses was solved by Maytag, an Iowa washing machine manufacturer, who used war-surplus shell-making machinery

Car bodies moved along on rollers while workmen put the upholstery in place.

A.M.A.

MESSY JOB
Before painting techniques were modernized, finishing off the body was a particularly messy job. These men are finishing car bodies by allowing varnish to flow over the surface.

A.M.A.

to make tubs out of metal, rather than wood. This method was successfully applied to car bodies. The combined experimentation revolutionized the body business.

Men worked, hour after hour, wet to the skin, smoothing the metal surface of car bodies with hand sanding blocks. Even though water cascaded over the metal surfaces, metal finishing of the bodies-in-white was extremely dusty. As a result it was conducted in great plants far removed from painting operations. After the metal finishing, the body-in-white was given a primer coat to prevent rust, then was hauled by the body truck across town to the paint shop. From there it was trucked elsewhere to acquire its trim, upholstery, hardware and glass. At last it was taken to the final assembly line to be fitted to a chassis, ready to move another step nearer the impatient customer.

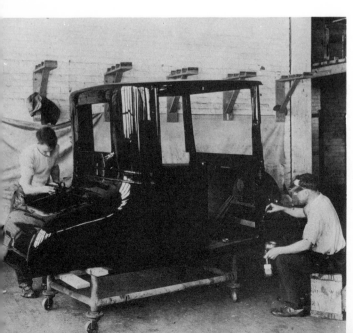

The time required to paint car bodies by hand presented a severe headache to the oft-prodded production departments.

General Motors Photographic

A.M.A.

DROPPING THE PILOT
The Model T, symbol of an age that was passing, dropped from automotive production annals in June, 1927. Neither chassis nor engine had been substantially altered for fifteen years. Finally Chevrolet began to push Ford for first place. Henry Ford, having seen his 15,000,000th car produced, announced: "The Model T has been a pioneer but conditions in the industry have so greatly changed that further refinement is now desirable." He shut down shortly, and went to work on a new car, the Model A.

BATTLE OF THE TITANS

Henry Ford's "Tin Lizzie," butt of more jokes than a legion of farmers' daughters, steadily outdistanced its competitors. In 1923, Ford manufactured 2,055,906 motor vehicles, while the rest of the industry combined produced 4,034,000 cars and trucks. GM's Charles Franklin Kettering, toastmaster at an Automobile Show dinner in New York, at which Ford was not represented, blinked through his glasses and cracked:

"When I look around this vast ballroom, packed to the rafters with company officials, and realize you account for only 50 per cent of the industry's production and sales, it makes me wonder how large a hall Mr. Ford hires when he puts on a dinner."

Sitting in the audience was a big-boned Dane, William S. Knudsen, once Ford's production manager, but now with Chevrolet. Currently he was instilling new vitality into an organization, whose product Ford was outselling thirteen to one. Sensing that the public desired style and performance in a low-priced car, Knudsen dolled up the Chevrolet, increased its horsepower, lengthened its wheel base. At dealer meetings, when the hulking Dane rose to his feet, he made the same speech. Holding up a finger on each hand, he'd insist, "I vant von for von." Then he'd sit down to a roar of applause from the distribution men who understood clearly what he meant—one Chevrolet must be sold for every Ford sold.

The changing tastes of America played into Chevrolet's hands. The Model T failed to satisfy the pride of ownership which motorists began to crave. Keeping up with the Joneses demanded a car with more flair and individuality, and some color other than black. Hardening of the arteries slowly set in, sales declined for three successive years after 1923, and the Model T, despite a brief effort to restyle it, was doomed. When Ford shut down for six months in 1927, preparatory to launching the Model A, Chevrolet sprinted ahead, passing both Ford and the million-car mark for the first time. Chevrolet's emergence as industry leader was particularly gratifying to General Motors president Alfred P. Sloan. A few years earlier he chose to disregard a survey made by a firm of management consultants, which had recommended dropping Chevrolet entirely from the GM family.

118

Albert Russel Erskine, then president of Studebaker, poses confidently by his President Eight Roadster, which had paced the 1929 Indianapolis Speedway Race. At the wheel is Studebaker production chief, Harold S. Vance. At his right is Paul G. Hoffman, then sales manager, who four years later succeeded to Studebaker's presidency. The company also produced the Erskine car.

Studebaker Corp.

In the great automotive sweepstakes of the twenties, contestants were plentiful and the competition was torrid. At the 1921 National Automobile Show there had been eighty-seven car exhibitors. The number dropped to forty-six at the end of the decade.

The smaller companies kept crowding the bigger makers through exercise of ingenuity, styling, mechanical improvements and frequent innovations. One of the oldest independent companies was Studebaker, then considered large by the standards of the times (one of 963 firms in the nation employing more than a thousand men), but not particularly big in automotive terms. In 1923, Studebaker received more money for its cars than for all the horse-drawn vehicles and harnesses sold in the sixty-eight years it had engaged in that business.

Its car sales in 1923 had amounted to a thumping $160,000,000. The following year Albert Russell Erskine, who had come from the typewriter business, got the idea while traveling abroad of bringing out a new small car, the Erskine Six. Oddly, it made its first appearance not in South Bend, but in Paris at the French Automobile Show. Erskine sold the car abroad first, then introduced it to the American market. It was hailed as combining "refinement of body and the precision characteristics of European cars with the high standards of durability, comfort and performance of American cars."

Charles F. Kettering, the self-styled "monkey-wrench scientist," was asked to head the multi-million dollar GM Research Laboratory. Nearly all companies gave increased emphasis to research and engineering. A succession of significant developments showed up in the twenties: balloon tires, four-wheel brakes, all-steel closed bodies, Ethyl gasoline, hypoid gears, synchronmesh transmissions, down-draft carburetors, hydraulic brakes, high compression engines.

This manufacturers' exhibit held in Chicago in the twenties was jokingly referred to as "The Tombstone Show." The posts in the center, intended to be decorative, took up valuable exhibit space.

A.M.A.

Walter P. Chrysler poses with his low-priced Plymouth.

Chrysler Corp.

There were also some significant price developments. In 1924, Roy Chapin priced his new Essex models at $900 for the touring car, and only $100 more for the coach. This marked the first time a six-cylinder car was available for less than $1,000. But Chapin created a greater stir by keeping his closed and open Hudson models at the same price—$1,500. When the price disadvantage was removed from the closed model, the open car declined sharply in popularity. Eventually the open models became almost extinct in America. Debut of the convertible a few years later was needed to revive the popularity of sitting unprotected in the great outdoors.

Development of the low-priced closed car contributed to the growing car demand. The owner no longer had to jack up his car on its four wheels for the winter. The automobile became more of a year-round family vehicle. And the dealers found they could talk a prospect into making a down-payment even in the late fall.

Other manufacturers followed Chapin's example of marking down the price of closed cars. In 1925, Alvan Macauley, who had gone from Burroughs Adding Machine Co. into Packard, lopped $800 off his sedan and watched sales spurt as never before. Peerless cut the price of its coupe

William S. Knudsen, center, restyled the Chevrolet, dropped its price to $607, and started out after Ford's production and sales leadership. In five years Knudsen caught up with his one-time boss, Henry Ford.

120

from $2,950 to $2,495. Pierce-Arrow introduced a $3,000 model, lowest in its history. In the popular-priced class, Willys-Overland slashed its selling figure to $595, a price only $15 above the Ford sedan.

The public responded enthusiastically to the bargains. By September, a shortage of cars threatened. New models virtually had disappeared, and dealers were down to an average of six cars apiece, most of them used models. Sales continued high throughout the fall, and the year ended on a record production of 3,735,000 passenger cars, more than a half million units above the previous year.

Another gladiator now had entered the battle of titans. Walter P. Chrysler, an ex-railroad mechanic who had climbed via Buick to the executive vice presidency of General Motors, came out in 1924 with the Chrysler Six. The Automobile Show that year wouldn't accept the new car for showing because it hadn't been in production long enough. Undaunted, Chrysler took space down the street at the Commodore Hotel. It attracted more attention than many of the makes at the show itself. The following year the new Chrysler 70 (so called because of its maximum speed in miles per hour) became the talk of the show. Its speed and styling appealed to the smart young set. Proceeding with characteristic drive and vigor, Chrysler jumped his company to fourth place in the industry by 1928, when he acquired the Dodge Brothers organization. He soon brought out a $670 Plymouth coupe to invade the low-priced field. The race for supremacy among the motor makers was on.

Charles F. Kettering, head of General Motors Research, relaxed from scientific endeavors by taking his family on a 10,-000-mile journey through the West. The coach, "Miss Ohio," was equipped by "Boss Ket" with radio, phonograph, tents, kitchen equipment and other comforts for the modern traveler of the twenties. Kettering, whose research endeavors for G.M. hastened the decline of Ford's Model T, was a fast friend of Henry Ford.

JAM 'EM IN
The land was loaded with automobiles. Three families out of four
had a car. The comforts of sitting
on the veranda had given way to
fighting for a parking space miles
from home. Here we see a Saturday
football crowd in the twenties.
A.M.A.

HIGH TIMES

A shrewd Midwesterner, talking with two Columbia University sociol-
ogists in 1925, asked:

"Why on earth do you need to study what's changing this country?
I can tell you what's happening in just four letters—A-U-T-O!"

Taking heed of the remark, Robert S. Lynd and Merrell Lynd discern-
ingly inspected Muncie, Indiana, the test tube for their famous sociological
study, *Middletown*. Among working-class families who furnished them
data, nearly one-half owned cars. The family car was a source of considerable pride. "We'd rather do without clothes than give up the family car,"
a mother of nine children reported.

In rural areas, a similar situation prevailed. When an investigator for
the Department of Agriculture asked a farm wife why the family owned a
car when it didn't own a bathtub, the woman replied with surprise:

"Why, you can't go to town in a bathtub!"

A foreign visitor to Detroit, glancing out of a factory window at the
workers' parking lot, exclaimed:

"Is it possible that you have that many executives working here?"

America had taken to wheels in a big way. Backyards were cut down
in size to make way for the garage. The front porch now was deserted on
Sunday afternoon, while the highways were jammed. The pattern of living,
working and playing was undergoing a tremendous change in the decade
after the war.

About three families out of four had automobiles at the end of the
decade. More than 23,000,000 passenger cars were on the road—16,000,000
more than at the beginning of the period. The public had spent nearly
thirty billion dollars on new automobiles in ten years.

Four out of five new car sales involved trading in the old vehicle. These
used cars then passed into the hands of others needing personal transportation, so that the circle of car ownership steadily widened. Car ownership

The factory girls sported permanent waves, their boy friends new roadsters. This Studebaker woman stitches upholstery.

Studebaker Corp

had become a necessity in the typical American family's scale of values.

American automobile factories developed a thriving business abroad. Their agents were sent around the world with motion pictures to lecture on how America's living standards were by-products of automotive and highway development. Thousands of new jobs were created in Midwestern factories to supply parts and equipment for Bombay, Capetown, Rio and other assembly centers for finished American vehicles. It was reported that one automobile job out of ten was related to the export trade.

The automobile business was becoming highly competitive. Prices were shaved to catch a big proportion of the market. In 1926, Willys-Overland realized a profit of only $10 per car, having decided that a low profit margin but a high volume provided the formula most worthwhile to stockholders. The following year John Willys brought out the Whippet Six, priced it at $795, and sold the car in trainloads. In 1928, his touring car prices were dropped to $615, which allowed him to advertise that his makes were "the lowest priced sixes in the world."

Walter P. Chrysler now had Plymouth in the low-priced field, Dodge in the medium and DeSoto and Chrysler in the upper price brackets. With the extensive Dodge manufacturing facilities now at his disposal, he was making a valiant and increasingly successful bid for third place in the production race.

At the beginning of 1929, William S. Knudsen, Chevrolet's chief, introduced a six-cylinder car to further the intense competition with Ford.

Chevrolet

The "era of wonderful nonsense" produced many giddy photographs designed to catch the tabloid editor's eye. One automobile publicist posed the Halwick dancers in an almond orchard scene entitled "Spirit of Spring." Star of the Tableau, of course, was the Studebaker 1928 President.

Henry Ford's Model A, presented to the public after a six months shutdown on his plants, created a considerable stir. While lacking elegance of looks, it had twice the engine power as its predecessor and sold for about the same price as the Model T. Ford had more than 100,000 men and women working in Detroit alone. It was necessary to make every day a "Pay-Day" at the River Rouge plant in order to pay off all employes without long line-ups and unnecessary strain on the paymaster's department. With high wages prevailing, Ford's own workers constituted a big market for his $495 two-door sedans. As it required another half-year for Ford to attain volume production on Model A, Chevrolet continued to keep ahead in 1928.

Realizing that Ford's production problems were about solved, the competition decided to offer more value to the customers. At the close of the season, Chevrolet announced that its 1929 cars would be six-cylinder cars. And, added general manager William S. Knudsen, at no advance in price. The price of the six-cylinder car dropped under the $600 mark for the first time. In a tremendous spurt of effort, automobile plants in 1929 produced 5,651,000 cars and trucks, the most staggering total in the industry's history up to that time, and a record which was to stand for another twenty years. However, danger signals were posted that the production rate was getting ahead of demand. New cars moved slower that spring in the Southwest and on the Pacific Coast. Poor weather at first was held to blame, but by August, the rate of production was cut. Then on October 26, the big crash occurred on the New York Stock Market. In December automobile production dropped to the lowest point for any December since 1921. The period of seemingly unlimited prosperity had come to an abrupt end.

GRIM OUTLOOK

President Hoover shows his growing concern over the slumping national economy. Declines in industrial activity, farm income, exports, all foreshadowed a period of depression. Following the economic curve, automobile production slumped sharply. Mileage traveled by cars, however, continued to rise throughout the thirties.

Akron Studio

LOW BUDGETEERS

By the thirties, income had ceased to be a criterion of car ownership. Farm families with annual cash incomes as low as $250 still had cars. The roads swarmed with hand-me-downs — rickety, rusting, decrepit cars that could be coaxed into running a few more miles. By using these tired old mechanisms, a horde of displaced farm people lugging along their household belongings swarmed across the Western mountains into California. This exodus from Oklahoma and surrounding areas fastened a new term on migrant automobilists of the period — Okies.

Chapter 4

THE JOADS OVERTAKE THE JONESES (1930-1940)

DIMINUENDO

THE DECADE of superlatives gave way to one of diminutives. Within three years of the 1929 peak, nearly everything was smaller, and cheaper.

Wages were down 60 per cent, salaries 40 per cent, farmers' cash income $4.4 billion.

Trains were shorter, Pullman cars fewer, passengers and tips scarcer.

The automobile companies found they had only one customer in 1932 for every four in 1929. Not that the people didn't want cars. A third quarter report in 1932 showed that 9,068 cars had been sold in Chicago and 10,199 stolen in the same period.

For a brief moment, it appeared that even passenger cars would get smaller. When the Austin came onto the market, a Bridgeport service station operator winced and hung up a sign:

> AUTOMOBILES WASHED, $1.00; AUSTINS DUNKED,
> 25 CENTS.

But like the national economy, the midgets didn't enjoy a prosperous life. If Americans could buy a new car at all, they wanted a type that didn't provoke jibes. Nor did the sixteen-cylinder Cadillac, planned in prosperity and introduced in 1930, appear to be the thing to drive just now.

In 1931, many motorists never set foot inside a new car. One group of show girls, however, for publicity purposes, crowded into the back seat of a Nash Phaeton parked outside Loew's Theatre in New York. The car sold for $895, and enabled its manufacturer to turn a profit in 1932, the only independent car maker who did. *Nash Motors*

Contrary to the economic trend, filling stations showed no appreciable drop in business. People continued to drive, even though jobless. In Moline, Illinois, a Tri-City relief committee ruled against making food handouts to people who had cars. They jotted down license plate numbers to determine whom to disqualify, but quickly dropped this on discovering that people preferred going without food to giving up their cars. In Muncie, the Lynns, checking again on "Middletown's" habits, reported: "People give up everything in the world but their cars."

Relief agencies recognized, too, that their clients' mobility had economic value. Unemployed motorists, able to get out into the country, picked up food which otherwise would have rotted in the fields. Cars could haul firewood to unheated homes. By having a car to transport ladders and buckets, an enterprising reliefer could scour the town for house painting and cleaning jobs.

Despite bad times, millions of dollars of unpaid balances were met on installment sales of cars. Repossession of cars increased only from 3 per cent in 1929 to 3.7 per cent in 1930, and dropped to 2.7 per cent in 1935. The proportion of installment sales to total sales remained about the same: 61 per cent in 1929 and 1930, 63 per cent in 1931, 58 per cent in 1935.

But customers for new cars became, in total numbers, SMALLER and Smaller and smaller:

Year	Domestic Sales
1929	4,136,000
1930	2,537,000
1931	1,839,000
1932	1,062,000

Exports dropped, too, to a piddling 73,115 cars in 1932. In 1929, when nearly one car out of five was sold abroad, automobile exports had totaled 451,000 units. When the depression became world-wide, foreign countries which had automobile industries increased their tariffs and slapped quota limitations on American-made cars. The declining markets at home and abroad took their toll among automobile producers.

Walter P. Chrysler drove his millionth Plymouth off the production line in 1934, a year in which his company managed to double its 1929 output. Shaking hands with the boss is B. E. Hutchinson, chairman of the board at Plymouth.

Plymouth

BID FOR CUSTOMERS

The 1931 National Automobile Show found only thirty-six manufacturers exhibiting their products. In 1929 there had been fifty-three and in 1921 a total of eighty-seven exhibitors.

In the fight for the favor of the vanishing supply of customers, most companies slashed prices. As their volume was down, this action had its effect on company profits, too. In 1930, Chrysler made fewer dollars than he made automobiles—a net of $234,000 on 267,000 cars. This amounted to a profit of eighty-nine cents per car! But he got sales. The following year, Chrysler sold more cars than all other companies combined in the so-called independent class.

Henry Ford started out bucking the depression with a flurry of activity. In December, 1929, he raised his minimum wage from $6 to $7 a day. He cut the price of his Model A coupe from $525 to $490. Gobbling up a big share of the market, he took the lead away from Chevrolet. But in 1931 Ford's sales fell to only half of the previous year's, and Chevrolet romped back into Number One position. Late in the year Ford announced that he was bringing out an eight-cylinder car. Ford's Model A was giving up in four years, while the Model T had enjoyed a nineteen-year life span. When the Ford V-8 arrived with a $490 price tag on the coupe, Chevrolet promptly marked its model down to the identical price.

With his sights still on getting Plymouth into the same league with Ford and Chevrolet, Chrysler introduced a six-cylinder Plymouth in November, 1932. He priced it at $495 for the coupe. There now definitely were three major contenders for the low-cost field.

Hudson also cut the price of its Essex to compete in the race, but it did poorly. In 1932, Roy Chapin replaced his one-time favorite with the smallish Terraplane. Offering it at $475 in the coupe model, Hudson undersold all competing new makes.

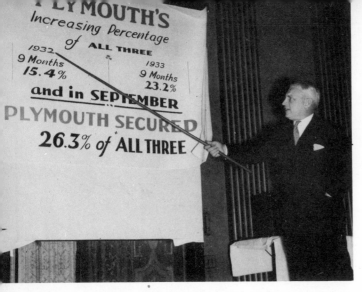

When the Whippet couldn't stand the competitive gaff, it was dropped; Willys-Overland's new line called the Willys had a rocky time in the sales mart. Graham-Paige was bidding for a share of the market with a $785 model known as the "Prosperity Six," which failed to bring financial blessing back to the company.

In fact, all the independents suffered deficits in 1932, except Nash, which had steadily realized a profit on its lines. The automobile industry had reached a very low ebb. The industry's total production had a wholesale value of $754 million against $3.4 billion just three years previously.

RECOVERY

There were some encouraging elements in the economic picture. For one thing, old cars were going off the road at a rate greater than new ones were being built. This pointed to potential sales just to meet replacement needs. Another significant economic, as well as social fact, was that decentralization of cities had continued during the depression. The areas surrounding metropolitan cities were increasing in population at three times the rate within city limits. In fact, the automobile was credited by the President's Research Committee on Social Trends in 1933 with having "erased the boundaries which formerly separated urban from rural territory and has introduced a type of local community without precedent in history." The private automobile supplied the transportation link that made such supercommunities possible.

In the spring of 1933, a more optimistic attitude toward the future swept over the land. A change in the national Administration took place along with a resurgence of economic activity here and abroad. In May, 1933, automobile retail sales managed to reach a higher level than those for the corresponding month the year before. As it had been forty-two months since this had happened, the economists cheered. When the year ended, the industry still wasn't prosperous but it had sold 438,000 more cars than the previous year.

Packard president Alvan Macauley and son Edward stand by a $2900 Packard at the National Show in 1937. Two years before Packard brought out an eight-cylinder model priced at $1,000, and sold five times as many cars as in 1934.

Akron Studios

Unfortunately, though, two companies, Willys-Overland and Studebaker, had gone into receivership during the year. The makers of fine automobiles, such as Duesenberg, Pierce-Arrow and Franklin, had rough going and their end was near. One favorite of sports style lovers, the Stutz, died of financial constriction early in 1933. Before its last gasp, however, the company contributed the 100-mile-an-hour Super Bearcat, whose lines and performance evolve nostalgia among the sporting clan today.

Employment, payrolls and production all began to rise in 1934. Jobs in auto plants increased to 273,000 from 190,000, and payrolls spurted from $233,500,000 to $372,000,000. Total passenger car output rose to 2,177,919 units, or 38 per cent above the previous year. Cars in the medium priced field, such as Dodge, Oldsmobile and Pontiac, benefited from the upturn in conditions. Packard decided to get into that bracket, and in 1935 brought out a $1,000 car, called the Packard 120. An eight-cylinder, 3,700 pound car, it was capable of ninety miles an hour speed. Motorists who had long yearned to drive this aristocratic make, but had found their $2,500 to $3,000 prices prohibitive, got their opportunity to switch to Packard when the price came down. Packard sold 36,700 cars, more than five times what it sold in 1934.

Posing with two Plymouth officials is Frank Murphy, in white suit, who was mayor of Detroit during the early days of the depression and governor of Michigan during the 1937 sitdown strikes.

Drucker-Hilbert

The Chrysler salon in 1937 gave evidence that a touch of elegance was once more acceptable in car merchandising. Among the depression casualties was the Stutz car, below, which expired in 1933. Here is the Stutz Super-Bearcat, powered with 32-dual-valve double overhead camshaft and a 32-valve engine. It was capable of 100 miles an hour.

A popular feature of the thirties was the car radio. A limited number had been sold on expensive cars in the late twenties, but as the price came down their use increased greatly. This picnic party enjoyed music through a loud-speaker connected with the automobile radio by an extension cord.

Studebaker quickly emerged from receivership. Plymouth's big output helped Chrysler Corporation double its 1929 production. Ford took the lead away from Chevrolet again. The industry wound up 1935 by making 3,252,244 cars, giving it the best year since 1929. Hope began to surge anew in the auto-makers' breast. The auto worker, too, began to perk up at the increasing production and profits. Efforts to unionize the workers, which had begun under the banner of NRA's Blue Eagle, proceeded at a faster and bolder pace.

SITDOWNS

Output again rose in the automobile industry in 1936. General Motors production on a world-wide basis reached the best level in its history. Plymouth's sales spurted to nearly 500,000 cars. Ford, however, showed a decline. Nash again had a profitable year, merged with Kelvinator, and ended up with a new president, George W. Mason. Willys-Overland reorganized, and emerged from under the jurisdiction of the court. The National Automobile Show changed its date to November, in an effort to give a boost to the fall selling season and level out the season dip in employment. But labor unrest broke out in a rash of strikes, interfering with production of tires, plate glass, aluminum, frames and other parts. The United Auto Workers, now under the banner of John L. Lewis' newly organized CIO, staged a sitdown strike at Bendix, a major supplier. On December 30, a similar tactic closed the Fisher Body plant at Flint, and spread rapidly until twenty General Motors plants were closed by strike. This device of workers locking themselves in company plants attracted nation-wide attention, and resulted in a long controversy over the legality of the action. The strike ended in February with General Motors recognizing the U.A.W. as the bargaining agent for its members, but not as the exclusive bargaining agent.

The U.A.W. then went after Chrysler to get exclusive bargaining agreement. Negotiations broke up on March 8 and a seventeen day sitdown strike ensued.

A plague of such strikes swept Detroit that spring, spread to other parts of the country and to other industries. The union finally won an exclusive bargaining agreement at Packard and got concessions from others. At Ford, however, it ran into a stonewall of opposition which continued until 1941, when the company did a complete about-face and gave the union the most sweeping labor contract written in the industry up to that time. Detroit, long a staunch open shop town, within five years had become the nation's Number One union town.

SUSPENDED PRODUCTION

In 1937 the nation's attention was focused on a dramatic new technique in union bargaining — the sitdown strike. The workers locked themselves in the plant and defied management to do anything about it. Here is a peaceful interlude in the long strike staged by the United Auto Workers (CIO) at the Fisher Body Plant No. 3 in Flint, Michigan, early in 1937. At right, Ford Motor Company was the last stronghold of the open shop. Ford did not sign with the United Auto Workers until 1941. Here is the employees' parking lot at Ford in the thirties.

Farm Security Administration

A.M.

General Motors

MILESTONE

In January, 1940, General Motors observed the production of the 25th million car to be made on its production lines. The top brass gathered in the Flint Chevrolet plant as the designated anniversary car got its windshield adorned with white paint. In the center is William S. Knudsen, president of General Motors. At his right is Alfred P. Sloan, chairman, and M. E. Coyle, Chevrolet general manager. Four months later Mr. Knudsen left his General Motors post and went to Washington to lend his talents to the defense production program.

UP AGAIN, DOWN AGAIN

Despite the prolonged strikes, production in 1937 was the best for any year of the decade—3,916,000 passenger cars and 893,000 motor trucks.

On the heels of rising wage and material costs came an increase in car prices. Except for Willys, which had a $499 coupe, the bracket below $500 had been wiped out. Ford increased prices from $530 to $595, Plymouth from $580 to $595, and Chevrolet from $615 to $648. Prices on cars in the middle and upper price brackets, too, reflected the higher cost of doing business. Before the year was over, however, an economic recession swept over the nation, and new car sales began to suffer. By the end of the first three months of 1938, production was off one-half the previous year's rate; second quarter output was even worse. Recovery set in late in the year, and while the automobile business kept step accordingly, it ended the year with total car output for the year down by 1,915,000 cars. Percentage-wise, production was off 48 per cent from the year before. The sale of used cars, however, held to within 70 per cent of the 1937 mark. Good times or bad, people demonstrated they still would buy transportation in some form.

Carl Byoir & Associates Crosley introduced pre-war a small car. This 1939 Crosley Cabriolet was 56 inches high, 47 inches wide and 120 inches long. It weighed 975 pounds, and operated 50 miles on a gallon of gasoline.

Two new cars appeared in 1939. Studebaker invaded the low-price field with its light weight, $660 Champion. Powell Crosley, Jr., the radio manufacturer, broke into the automobile field with a 925-pound Crosley car, priced at $325. Another car, Ford's Mercury, while introduced the previous summer, made its first real bid for the market in 1939, ended up in ninth place in the selling lists. The industry as a whole regained about half the ground it lost in the 1938 recession, and closed with a passenger car volume of 2,866,800 units.

Outbreak of war in Europe in September had no immediate effect on the industry. A month later the Automobile Manufacturers Association by action of its directors declared itself "unreservedly opposed to participation by the United States in the present European war." The following May, however, one of its important directors, William S. Knudsen, was called to Washington by President Roosevelt to serve on the National Defense Advisory Committee. By Automobile Show time in October, 1940, the last manufacturers' show the industry was to hold, the companies voluntarily agreed to forego tooling on new models in order to free capacity for the manufacture of defense tools. A few weeks later, the industry organized an Automotive Committee for Air Defense. Orders for military trucks and other vehicles began to be placed by Britain and France. Chrysler started work on a tank plant, Ford began making air-cooled aircraft engines, the Allison engine division of General Motors undertook to make liquid-cooled aircraft motors.

Under the stimulus of an expanding economy, Americans in 1940 purchased 3,608,000 new passenger cars. By now, the American public had 27,372,397 automobiles plying the streets and highways.

136

Evidence of how these cars were being used came from many parts of the nation. In Boston, an old city before the advent of the automobiles, 500,000 people entered the downtown area by car. Subways, streetcars, buses, railroads and ferries all combined carried not quite 900,000 passengers. Los Angeles, a newer metropolis, reported that 56 per cent of the people traveled by private passenger car to get downtown. In the smaller cities, as many as 80 per cent of the people got into the central part of the city by private car. In Midland, Michigan, this figure reached 91.8 per cent, causing one writer to comment: "Without his automobile the average Midlander's plight would be about as sorry as that of a Laplander without his reindeer."

America now had one car for every 4.3 persons. As Americans entered a new phase of their history—production to feed a two-front war—it began to dawn on them that this transportation pool was going to have to last for some time. For the factories were chewing up metal for defense weapons at a high rate, leaving a lesser amount for new automobiles. In the months ahead, civilian car production was destined to be limited, then completely curtailed.

At the beginning of the defense effort, America had one automobile for every 4.3 persons in the nation.

Free Lance Photographers Guild

REDUCED SPEED

Rural roads became free of the Sunday driver who now had to stay home to conserve his gasoline supply, his tires and his car. The government banned speeds above 35 miles per hour as part of its conservation program. So many "Out of Gas" signs, below, dotted the landscape that motorists began following petroleum trucks to get a few gallons of fuel.

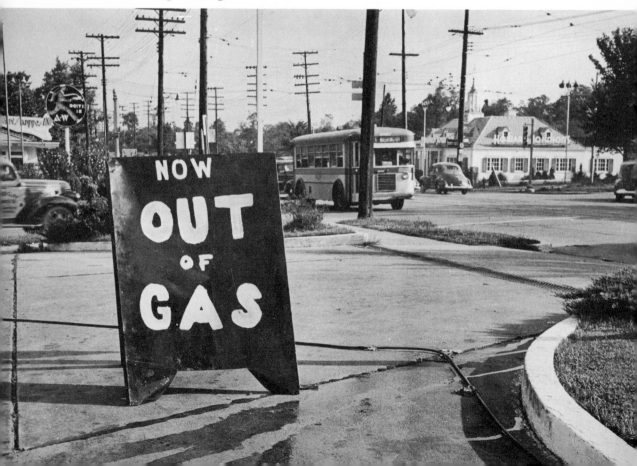

Chapter 5

WORLD AT WAR (1941-45)

CONFUSED TIMES

AUGHT in a swirl of international developments, Americans remained
confused in mind and divided in spirit throughout most of 1941. Debate raged in Congress and around countless cracker barrels over aid
to Britain, Lend-Lease, new powers placed in the Presidency, and other
vital issues. Strikes at home and battle news from Europe competed for
headlines. Congress in August managed to extend military conscription by
a single vote majority. In September, President Roosevelt ordered the Navy
to "shoot on sight" Axis ships threatening the United States. On the last day
of October, an American First Committee isolationist rally in New York
attracted 20,000 people. In November, Congress voted to change the Neu-
trality Act, John L. Lewis ordered coal miners to strike, and Secretary of
State Cordell Hull handed diplomat Saburo Kurusu terms under which
the United States would continue peace discussions with the Japanese
Government.

As the tempo of American life stepped up, the American motorist
morning and evening switched on his car radio for news reports. Over it
came a series of announcements affecting his ability to buy, repair, finance,
admire or use automobiles.

In January, the auto manufacturers announced they were calling off
the 1941 Auto Show because they were too busy on defense work to hold
one. In February, the Government ordered conservation of aluminum,
nickel and other critical materials needed for car-building. In April, auto
makers met with Knudsen, now head of the Office of Production Management, and agreed to reduce their output 20 per cent.

Taking over the nation's rubber supply in June, the Government reduced civilian consumption by 20 per cent, froze tire prices, banned the
manufacture of white sidewall casings. In August, the car makers eliminated the chrome strips and other trim that brightly decorated their new
models. Early in September installment credit controls regulated the customer's purchasing of cars. Production of light trucks came under Government limitation orders on September 13. Two days later, passenger car
manufacturers were ordered to cut their production quotas in half. In
quick succession came Government limitation orders on spare parts and
motor fuels.

DOUBLE DUTY

As did many service men and civilians, automobile plant personnel strained under a big double load. Engineers and metallurgists tussled with the problem of finding satisfactory substitutes for critical metals that were getting scarcer by the week. Top priority was given, however, to their defense production assignments. As an industry, they had worked cooperatively on a bomber production program, until the job could be assigned to individual producers. That done, Ford broke ground, early in the year, for a bomber plant at Willow Run, Michigan, to make the Consolidated warplanes. General Motors assigned production of the North American bomber to its Fisher division, and Chrysler and Hudson teamed up with Goodyear to make the Martin B-26 bomber.

Packard turned out the marine engines destined to speed General Douglas MacArthur via PT boat from beleaguered Bataan the following year. Hudson broke ground for a naval arsenal. Scarcely a month went by without the awarding of an aircraft engine order. Studebaker, Nash, Buick, Ford, Chevrolet, all undertook sizable assignments. General Motors' Steering Gear division at Saginaw built its first machine guns in March, 1941. Chrysler delivered its first tank to the Army in April. Nash took on an airplane propeller assignment in May. Bofors cannon now began to come off one production line, reconnaissance cars rolled from another. After ten months' advance preparation, Packard completed its first Rolls-Royce airplane engine in August. Ford produced, tested and delivered its initial Pratt & Whitney engine. Orders trickled through from Washington for Oerlikon guns, submarine chasers, mine sweepers, searchlights, shells, radar equipment. By the first of December, the cumulative defense work placed since 1939 with the automotive industry reached $4 billion.

"Rosie the Riveter" took her place cheerfully alongside factory men to help wage the Battle of Production.

Hudson Motor Co.

140

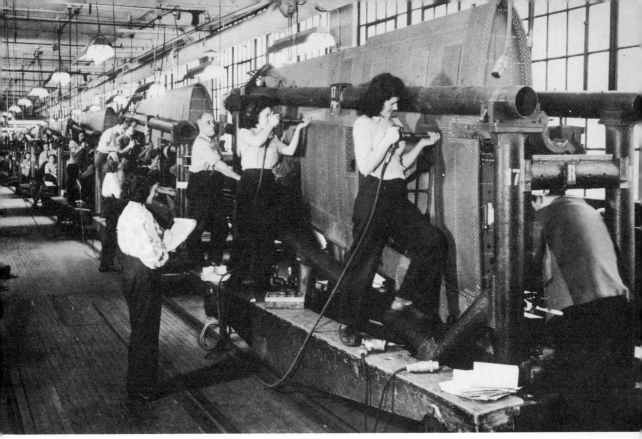

Hudson Motor Co.

RIVETS AWAY

Workers of 33 nationalities shouldered rivet guns to help produce Curtiss Helldiver airplane wings on this 5,618-foot-long Hudson Motor Company assembly line. In the hands of the Navy, the Helldiver bomber helped turn the tide against the Japs at Rabaul.

CALL TO ARMS

Then on Sunday morning, December 7, 1941 Japanese planes droned over the Island of Oahu, dropped bombs on the navy base at Pearl Harbor, crippled the American Pacific fleet, and killed 2,117 soldiers, sailors and civilians. The sneak attack united 132 million Americans, and wiped out the indecision, delay and debate over the nation's rearmament program.

On December 8, telephone circuits between Washington and Detroit, South Bend, Lansing, Flint, Pontiac, Dayton, Cleveland, Kenosha and other automotive centers were jammed. Long distance calls reached all-time peaks as military officials released a flood of new assignments.

In the next five weeks, the War Department alone contracted for three and one-half billion dollars of supplies, a total equal to all defense contracts given the industry in the first two years after the Nazi invasion of Poland.

In succeeding weeks the total grew until the industry's accumulated orders exceeded fourteen billion dollars—a production job calling for materials and men sufficient to produce 15,000,000 cars and trucks, normally a three years' job.

The New York Times observed:

> The American automobile industry, chief pride of a nation dedicated to mass production, low-cost economy, admittedly holds a most important card in the international poker game which will determine continuance of the American way.

The motorist felt the impact of the war almost immediately. OPM banned both the production and sale of tires. In Detroit, gangs of tire hijackers roamed the neighborhoods, stripped off the lugs, and made away with car wheel and all. Word got around that all this was unnecessary. You could cross the border into Canada and buy new tires freely.

Sales of new passenger cars and trucks were frozen on the first of the year, and a certificate of necessity was required to obtain one.

The Chicago Sun, like scores of other newspapers sent correspondents to the factory front, to report what was happening. On January 16 *The Sun* reported:

> All across the world, in Holland, Belgium, France, the Balkans; on the Siberian steppes, the winding stretches of the Burma Road, the vast Libyan deserts, the steaming settlements along the equator, the outposts up in the Arctic circle—millions of people, brown, yellow and white . . . are waiting.
>
> Old-timers tell you that the layoff always used to come in January when the plants took inventory, got set for the new models.
>
> But this year the New Models will not be automobiles. This year Detroit is tooling up for Armageddon.
>
> And the place names of River Rouge, Flint, Pontiac, Lansing, Toledo and South Bend have become the battle sites of the world's freedoms.

Four days later came a decisive action, affecting the supply of passenger cars. Donald Nelson ordered all civilian production of passenger vehicles halted completely. The deadline set was February 10.

A General Motors employees' parking lot became crowded with fender presses and other tools ripped from their factory moorings.

General Motors

THE BIG CHANGE-OVER

The nation's press reports the dramatic transformation of the automobile manufacturing industry to all-out war production.

A.M.A.

CONVERSION

Turmoil, demolition, reconstruction ensued in automobile plants in the early weeks of 1942. Conveyors were ripped out, machines uprooted and floors swept clean to make room for war work. Yards outside the plants were cluttered with huge single-purpose tools, moved into vacant lots to make room for specialized war production equipment. The acres of tools standing out in bitter Michigan weather gave the impression of behemoths frozen in the snow. Canvas covering afforded protection for some, heavy grease coated others. To find space for the idle equipment, one motor company converted its parking lot.

Elsewhere, master mechanics were frantically looking for other equipment to perform new and unaccustomed jobs. A tooling information service was set up within the industry to facilitate the search.

The motorist also had a search on his hands. With filling stations frequently running out of fuel, motorists followed gasoline trucks for blocks waiting to see where the driver was making his delivery. In May, gasoline rationing became effective in seventeen Eastern states. Before the year was up, it was made nation-wide. The Office of Defense Transportation ordered a thirty-five mile-an-hour speed limit for all rubber tired vehicles.

The Jeep apparently could go anywhere—even across a river on a cable. This photograph was taken during Second Army maneuvers near Camp Crowder, Missouri.

The Office of Price Administration froze the sale of all used tires and tubes. And the Government asked all drivers owning more than five tires to turn spares into the national stockpile. About one out of ten automobile dealers had gone out of business. Civilian truck production was stopped.

The outlook was getting pretty grim for the motorist when, shortly after Christmas, shipbuilder Henry J. Kaiser threw out a cheerful morsel. The West Coast producer announced that he planned to build a postwar car. The price, he said, would be around $500.

The automotive industry now was producing planes, tanks and guns at the rate of $20,000,000 daily. It had 960,000 people engaged in war work, which was a 26 per cent increase in total employment over its peacetime high in 1941. Many workers were new to the industry—married women, old men, the lame, the halt and even the blind. But despite material shortages, tooling delays, and loss of personnel to the armed forces, the industry had managed to produce $5.4 billion of arms and civilian goods in 1942.

TURN IN THE TIDE

For many a grim month, virtually nothing but bad news—of retreats, reversals, losses—emitted from the car radio. But a tide of armor, mobile units and airpower was surging steadily from U. S. factories. It began to have its effect. One of the first dramatic breaks came when Hitler's wily desert fox, General Erwin Rommel, encountered for the first time Detroit-made Sherman tanks, equipped with 105 howitzers. Their introduction on the Libyan front was a surprise to the British soldiers themselves—to say nothing of the Nazis. Lighter in weight than most tanks, and capable of speeds of 35 m.p.h.—ten miles faster than their predecessor—they helped General Sir Bernard Montgomery crumple Rommel's Panzer divisions and dissolve his fixed lines. The vaunted Afrika Korps started a 1,400 mile retreat across North Africa, with the Sherman tanks in hot pursuit. Rommel's desert army collapsed in May, 1943, giving the Allies their first decisive victory in four years. In July, Montgomery and General George Patton rolled their tanks, trucks and troops onto the Sicilian beaches, pressed on to Messina, and gained a springboard for invading Italy. Mussolini was imprisoned by his king, while the new premier Marshall Pietro Badoglio began dickering for peace.

HIGH TIDE

The production stream became swollen with automotive-made equipment, which helped turn the tide against the Axis powers. From the Chrysler tank arsenal above flowed the General Sherman tank which contributed to crushing Rommel's desert army in North Africa.

Automotive Council for War Production

First convoy over the Ledo-Burma road, linking China and India, parades through Kunming, China. Below, Marines push a jeep ashore during the invasion of Cape Gloucester in late 1943. Note litters for casualties to come.

The "pin-up" girl was exploited for conservation purposes at this Ledo Road refueling station.

U.S. Signal Corps

Across the world in Burma, a victory of another sort was in the making —the building of a 1,044 mile lifeline from India to China. For more than eighteen months, U. S. Army Engineers battled malaria, monsoon rains and Jap snipers to construct roads through Burmese jungles. Over them grunted and strained heavily-burdened American motor trucks delivering supplies to Lt. General Joseph W. Stillwell fighting in the Hukawng Valley. As soon as the first bulldozers cut a trail, motor vehicles began operations, carrying increasing amounts of machine guns, artillery, small arms, ammunition, clothing and other equipment to Chinese and American jungle troops facing the Japanese.

Jeeps traversed the New Guinea jungles to carry mail and supplies to the troops.

U.S. Signal Corps

U.S. Army Air Forces The cosmopolitan jeep, unruffled in the presence of the Sphinx, passes camel-borne U. S. airmen on a week-end outside Cairo. The Fifth Army, below, moves its big guns toward the front through the Porta Popolo in Rome in June, 1944.

President Roosevelt inspects American troops in Morocco where he went in early 1943 for the Casablanca conference with Churchill. In back seat is General Mark Clark.

U.S. Signal Corps

When the roads ran out, some vehicles still managed to get through. Two newspaper correspondents drove a jeep through the Chindwin jungles of Burma and over the Manipur hills to Imphal, India. On arrival at their destination, the officer in charge refused to believe them.

"Why, that's impossible, there isn't a single road across these jungles and hills," he snorted.

"Sh-h-h! Not so loud," cautioned one of the newsmen. "Our jeep hasn't found out yet about roads, and we don't want to spoil it!"

The chief of the Army's field service division, General Julian S. Hatcher, observing motor vehicles in action around the world, made this official report:

"Vehicles and roads used to grow up together," he wrote. "Now the Army asks only if there is traction or leverage, and if there is, we go in and fight."

Optimism mounted throughout 1944. Rabaul, key to Japan's superiority in the South and Southwest Pacific, fell to aerial bombardment, allowing MacArthur to eye hopefully the Philippines once again.

The people at home began to talk in terms that had long been stifled—peacetime plans. In February, 1944, Bernard Baruch announced a post-war program for America. In March, the War Production Board released materials for use in experimental models and test runs. Three months later the agency relaxed its material controls for the making of pilot models and permitted manufacturers to buy machinery for civilian production. General Motors announced it would expand production after the war by 40-50 per cent. Packard announced a 44 per cent boost in car output was contemplated. Ford denied a published news statement that the company planned a post-war version of its model "A". Patch-weary motorists got some authentic news—inner tubes were to be removed from rationing by early summer.

U.S. Signal Corps

MARS IN MOTION

At 4:15 A.M., Monday, June 5, 1944, General Dwight D. Eisenhower reviewed the latest weather information, heard the comments of his experts, then plunged into momentary silence as he pondered a decision of enormous consequences which he was about to make. He looked down the table in a conference room at Southwick Park, a country house near Portsmouth, England, and in a firm clear voice said to his staff commanders:

"All right, we move . . ."

Here is an amphibious Duck getting aboard an LST, bound for the invasion coast. Below are shown American tanks arriving at Cherbourg, where they were hastily serviced by Ordnance crews, then moved forward under their own power to railroads.

German defensive strategy was upset by American logistical devices such as the one-way "Red Ball Express" highway for top-priority motor convoys across France.

U.S. Signal Corps

WHEELS FOR INVASION

Concentrated in Britain meanwhile were the greatest number of military vehicles ever assembled. On June 5, they rolled endlessly toward embarkation ports to be loaded into LST's. Later that day General Dwight D. Eisenhower climbed into his Cadillac, drove from airfield to airfield, visiting paratroopers who were coloring their faces with cocoa and linseed oil. Toward evening the supreme commander climbed to the roof of a headquarters building to watch the Allies' planes roar southward toward the coast of France. Early the next morning, Eisenhower's order of the day rang into the ears of the assault troops headed for the Normandy beaches: "You are about to embark upon the great crusade. . ." D-Day had arrived.

On Wednesday, June 7—D plus one—Eisenhower crossed the Channel and from a mine layer watched the invasion forces in operation. A heavy surf pounded the beaches, increasing the difficulty of landing supplies and reinforcements. The sun peeped through the overcast. One writer reported that it "shone down on a long line of men and tanks and trucks, moving up and over the bluffs, moving in." Through a hell of gunfire they kept moving, moving, moving.

The Battle of the Beachhead won, supplies and reinforcements began flooding through Cherbourg and the artificial port near Arromanches. With

U. S. armored columns turn machine guns and light cannon on the Nazis who tried to outflank the Allies at Epernay, France.

thirty-six divisions in action, Eisenhower faced the problem of delivering 20,000 tons of supplies daily from the beaches and ports. His spearhead moved swiftly, covered up to seventy-five miles daily.

Despite fierce enemy counterattacks, the tide moved on. By the end of June, the Allies had more than 170,000 vehicles in Normandy. A second landing took place August 15 in the south of France. Four days later, the French Forces of the Interior, with aid from Eisenhower, liberated Paris. France was regained before summer's end.

The surge to the Rhine received an unexpected setback in the Ardennes forest in mid-December, when Hitler made an audacious gamble, threw his armored reserves against five U. S. divisions, and rent two great gaps in the lines. Gloom clouded many an American homefire that Christmas time until the news came through that Patton's and Montgomery's counterattack, valiantly supported by the Air Force, was wrecking General Karl Von Rundstedt's tanks and trucks right and left. The famous "Battle of the Bulge" soon ended in an overwhelming rout of the Von Rundstedt's troops. How decisive the turn proved to be was not generally apparent, but Hitler's confidant, General Kurt Manteuffel, later described it thusly:

"After the Ardennes failure, Hitler started a corporal's war. There were no big plans—only a multitude of piecemeal fights."

BLUEPRINT FOR VICTORY

At home, the automobile industry revealed in midsummer of 1944 that it had delivered $20 billion of war materials to the fighting forces. Willys Overland announced it had placed a contract for 25,000 bodies for postwar jeeps, to be produced as soon as the War Production Board allocated the materials. In September, automobile companies were permitted to put engineering personnel to work on postwar designs. Henry Ford II, now executive vice president of the Ford Motor Company, announced plans for a postwar car 15-20 per cent below the cost of the regular Ford. President Roosevelt, recently re-elected for a fourth term, signed Public Law 521 known as the Postwar Highway Construction bill.

Early in January, 1945, American troops invaded Luzon and headed for Manila. The Russians captured Warsaw. Roosevelt, Churchill and Stalin met at Yalta in February to discuss plans for postwar Germany.

DOWN HITLER'S ALLEY

Lt. General Brehon B. Sommerville, head of the Service of Supply, once said: "When Hitler hitched his chariot to an internal combustion engine, he opened up a new battle front — a front that we know well. Its called Detroit." By Spring of 1945, the truth of this statement was apparent to the world. Once Detroit-made chariots reached Hitlerland, they roared in high gear down the famous German autobahns. Here is a Third Army division sweeping toward Frankfurt, at a time when complete victory was in sight.

U.S. Signal Corps

Across the world in the Philippines, American military vehicles were moving in on the Japanese who burned their bridges behind them in their retreat from Olongapo, Luzon.

General Patton's Third Army soon reached the Rhine, drove his tanks miles inland. On the first of April, the U. S. invaded Okinawa, 325 miles to the south of Japan.

J. A. Krug, new head of the War Production Board, denied on April 5 that his agency had given the automobile industry permission to resume production of 250,000 passenger cars in the fall. He flew to Detroit, though, to discuss with industry leaders the necessary planning for peacetime production. The Office of Price Administration soon hinted at the possible increase in gasoline allowances after V-E Day. The WPB gave approval to the production of $50 million of machine tools for automobile production. With the Luftwaffe defeated, the Air Corps announced that the Willow Run bomber plant would close by August 1.

The radio, turned on in May, 1945, blared forth a series of stirring announcements. On May 2, President Truman, in his third week as the new occupant of the White House, announced the news of Adolph Hitler's death. Same day, Stalin proclaimed the capture of Berlin. On May 7, Germany surrendered unconditionally to the Allies.

RECONVERSION

With V-E Day passed, the WPB released steel, copper and aluminum for the production of civilian goods. In mid-May all restrictions were removed on the manufacture of spare parts for automobiles. The order forbidding bicycle production was revoked. The WPB gave the green light for the production of about 250,000 automobiles to start July 1 if materials could be obtained. Michigan Bell Telephone Company's postwar plans included telephone service to and from moving automobiles. Detroit celebrated "Knudsen Day" for Lt. General William S. Knudsen, who had just resigned from the Army and returned home after five years service with the government and military.

Getting the jump on its competitors, Ford cleaned out its River Rouge plant early, installed peacetime tools and managed to roll its first 1946 model off the assembly line on July 3. A few weeks later Henry Ford II gave one of the cars to President Truman. Before the month's end, too, Willys-Overland started production on the civilian version of the jeep, and OPA set a $1,090 price ceiling on the model. The 1946 model Oldsmobile went on display. Henry J. Kaiser and Joseph W. Frazer formed Kaiser-Frazer to build low and medium priced cars, and began negotiations to lease the Willow Run plant as their factory site.

At exactly fifteen minutes past 8:00 A.M. on August 6, 1945, Japanese time, an atomic bomb flashed above Hiroshima. It was released from a device manufactured in Detroit, and carried in a plane powered by engines built by Dodge in Chicago. A week and a day later, Japan surrendered.

Willys-Overland got into production on its first civilian jeep in mid-July, 1945. Known as the Universal model, this runabout resembled its wartime brother except for absence of rifle carrier and olive-drab paint.

Willys-Overland

WPB lifted all restrictions on passenger car production. Gasoline rationing was abolished. All manpower controls over workers and employers were dropped. The national wartime speed limit of thirty-five miles per hour was removed.

The war tools now were ripped out of the plants, and civilian tools moved back in. The scramble to get back into civilian passenger car, truck and bus production was on in earnest.

Meantime, industry statisticians took time out to tally up the war production totals. Automotive plants had contributed nearly $29 billion of war goods to the fighting forces. The output included:

Aircraft, aircraft subassemblies and parts	$11,216,487,000
Military vehicles and parts	8,612,173,000
Tanks and parts	3,808,626,000
Marine equipment	1,944,533,000
Guns, artillery and parts	1,587,736,000
Ammunition and components	909,335,000
All other war products	907,495,000
Total	$28,986,378,000

The industry's wartime organization, the Automotive Council for War Production, held a Victory dinner, then disbanded. Little time was spent on exultation. There was too much work to do. For American motorists, whose belts had been tightened for nearly four years, were ravenous for new passenger automobiles.

VICTORY DINNER

Packard chairman Alvan Macauley, who had headed the Automotive Council for War Production, gets a present in appreciation of his wartime services from the 1200 motor makers who attended the industry's Victory Dinner in Detroit in late 1945. Smiling their approval were Lt. General James D. Doolittle and William S. Knudsen, who five years before had affected "a wedding between the automotive and aircraft industries — without benefit of shotgun." Automotive companies produced $11 billion of completed aircraft and aircraft parts before the marriage was dissolved in 1945.

Automotive Council for War Production

Chapter 6

AMERICA IN MOTION

1945 TO THE PRESENT DAY

BRAVE NEW WORLD

BY THE TIME Mom's boy returned from the wars, the brave new world had a slightly cockeyed cast.

Instead of dream stuff as envisioned by the Sunday supplements, the old familiar styles were still around.

Instead of breadlines as forecasted, there were picket lines, jurisdictional disputes and work stoppages.

Instead of a plentiful supply of shiny new products, there were shortages. Steel, coal, electrical equipment and other items basic to car manufacture were in short supply. Only customers were in abundance.

Car production got off to a slow start. From July through October, 1945, only 19,136 passenger automobiles were produced—scarcely a day's production by the usual standards.

OPA, still clutching to its price control functions, allowed Ford a 6 per cent increase over its 1942 prices, plus "$30 for improvements." Even so, Henry Ford II, the new president, claimed the company was losing $300 on every Ford car produced, due to higher costs and low output.

The unions, restless after their wartime "no strike" pledge, demanded a 30 per cent wage increase. In the automobile industry, General Motors proposed to adjust wage rates to meet the increased cost of living. Walter Reuther, rising to power in the Auto Workers Union, rejected the offer, and on November 21, he struck General Motors.

True to advance billing postwar America did trot out some new gadgets.

The Virginia and Maryland Coach Company equipped its buses with two-way radios. Firestone announced a "blow-out proof" tire. Chevrolet took to television to plug its name.

Kaiser-Frazer moved into the Waldorf-Astoria in January, 1946, to display its hand-built models. Crowds clogged the sidewalks trying to get into the hotel. Inside, ropes held back enthusiasts who wanted to swarm over the new products.

In Chicago, Preston Tucker, formed a corporation to try to raise $40 million to build the "Tucker Torpedo," a rear engine car, with a Cyclops headlamp and crash-pads.

In Cincinnati, Crosley unveiled a light-weight 26½ h. p. model.

Studebaker caused a stir with a new modern design and got it into production early.

Most companies, however, placed new model plans on the "back burner," while they concentrated on piled-up orders for 1946 models. The Automobile Manufacturers Association in March canceled plans for a National Automobile Show, planned an Antique Car show instead.

The General Motors strike lasted 113 days, ended with workers granted a 18½ cents an hour wage increase. In April, John L. Lewis led 400,000 bituminous coal miners on a nation-wide strike, causing Ford to close a few weeks later. When wage negotiations reached a deadlock, a nation-wide railroad strike commenced. OPA raised the price ceilings of sixteen makes of cars from $33 to $67. Shortages of lead, copper, steel were becoming acute. Wartime controls still hung on. Detroit was groggy from months of strife, turmoil, confusion. Some thought it was an odd time to have a party. But Detroit and the automotive industry were determined to celebrate. While they were at it, they decided to hold a real whing-ding.

The war ended, Americans quickly got back into auto-motion again. In the past decade, faces of American cars hadn't changed much. Nor had the available space on U. S. streets. But more people were driving, or wanting to drive, than ever before. With gasoline rationing ended, the 5:30 "rush" hour had become more intolerable than ever. Here's the late afternoon Detroit traffic inching past General Motors Building. The corporation's headquarters became the focal point of national attention in late 1945, when its plants were struck and remained closed for 113 days.

General Motors

A.M.A.

JUBILEE PARADE
Detroit painted its streets gold to observe the "Golden Jubilee of the automotive industry." The year 1946 actually marked fifty years since Charles B. King, followed closely by Henry Ford, drove the first car in Detroit. Both men were on hand for the celebration, which was highlighted by a parade of about 300 old automobiles.

GOLDEN JUBILEE

They called it the Golden Jubilee. It had been exactly fifty years since Charles King and Henry Ford first operated gasoline cars on Detroit's streets. With few new models to show, the industry encouraged private collectors to comb museums, old barns and movie lots for antique cars and to converge on Detroit. A cavalcade of these creaking veterans sputtered down Woodward Avenue, gold painted for the occasion, while the camera recorded their colorful progress. At the end of the run, the ancient models were exhibited indoors for a week, so the old-timers could reminisce around them.

Under William S. Knudsen's general chairmanship, the industry staged a big banquet, climaxed by a "Tribute to the Pioneers." Gathered on the stage at Detroit's Masonic Temple were such veteran manufacturers as Ford, Nash, Olds, Duryea and Apperson, and several of the oldest workers, dealers and parts makers. Barney Oldfield, cigar and all, took bows as the pioneer race driver. All were given the "Clifton Award," the industry's equivalent of a movie "Oscar."

Trygve Lie, secretary-general of the United Nations, fondles the lamp of a
1910 Brush, while daughter Metta Lie and Jubilee general chairman William
S. Knudsen occupy the front seat.

George W. Mason, president of Nash-Kelvinator, and Charles E. Wilson, head of General Motors, sit in one of the ancient models while beamed upon by five young "models."

Tenor James Melton, antique car collector, drove his 1903 White Steamer in the Golden Jubilee parade.

Henry Ford and Barney Oldfield compared notes for the last time at the Golden Jubilee. At left are Alfred Reeves, pioneer showman, and grandson Benson Ford. To the right are Henry Ford II and George Romney, Jubilee manager.

Feeling like a freshman among seniors, Paul G. Hoffman walked up to a small group that included Henry Ford, Charles Nash and Frank Kwilinski, a veteran Studebaker worker being honored.

"Careful, there, Frank," jested Hoffman. "Remember you're among competitors."

"Don't you worry, Mr. Hoffman," said the onetime wagon maker, employed sixty years with the same company, "I'll never leave Studebaker."

A pretty Nash worker, known as the Jubilee Queen, pushed the button that produced the spark that lit the revolving downtown display—an old and new car encased in an atomic symbol. Unshaved from a dash across country in an antique car, singer Jimmy Melton arrived in time to sing *Wagon Wheels*. Trygve Lie flew out from the United Nations conference to speak at a "unity" rally at Briggs Stadium, where management and labor representatives smoked peace pipes together.

At the end of ten days of such goings on, Detroit felt better. Everyone went back to work in earnest. America, too, began to overcome some of its headaches, bottlenecks, impasses. In mid-December, the industry was permitted to install the spare tire again on new cars. At year-end, President Truman announced the official end of World War II hostilities, an action that automatically terminated the wartime emergency powers held by the Government.

The auto industry ended up the year producing 2,149,000 passenger cars—nearly thirty-three times the number turned out in the bobtail year of reconstruction that had preceded it.

UPWARD SPIRAL

The cockeyed world produced some wacky economic situations in 1947.

Parking lot rates in Detroit jumped overnight from thirty-five cents to ninety cents daily. Nationally, insurance companies upped liability rates for passenger cars 30 per cent, for trucks 40 per cent.

Used cars sold at higher prices than models fresh from the factory assembly lines.

Price reductions instituted by Ford, International Harvester and Plymouth lasted for some months, but before the year-end those three, too, joined all automobile and tire companies in pricing their products higher.

Excited about the possibilities of "portal-to-portal" pay, a group of industrial workers had their hopes crushed by District Judge Colin Neblett who ruled that time spent riding buses to and from work was not collectible.

Car-hungry Americans, impatiently waiting their turn on dealer wait-ing lists, fumed at the sight of brand-new cars being sold on used car lots. The Keystone Automobile Club reported that used car dealers were mark-ing up new models by as much as $1,000 over "legitimate dealer prices." The Philadelphia Automobile Trades Association started a drive against the resale of new cars for a premium. The National Automobile Dealers Association advised dealers to advertise the local delivered prices of new cars. Automobile companies tried to trace quick resales of their vehicles. One investigation trail led to the manse of a Chicago minister, who had written to various motor factories asking for help in getting a car to visit his flock; he was found to have sold eleven new cars at a tidy profit. A Detroit banker, favored with early delivery on a new limousine after seek-ing the intervention of an automobile company president was confronted with evidence that this car had shown up three days later on a Livernois Avenue used car lot. The banker hemmed, hawed, then admitted:

"Well, I really needed a new car, but when I was offered $300 more than I paid for this one, I just couldn't resist reselling it."

In Baltimore, the Circuit Court ruled that new cars must be dealt out according to dealers' waiting lists. The Detroit Automobile Dealers Asso-ciation urged dealers to get new buyers to sign contracts, pledging not to resell their new cars within six months. None of these actions did much good, however, as long as buyers outnumbered available products. In midyear, the Automobile Manufacturers Association stated that greater production was the only means of effectively checking the black market in new cars.

To overcome wartime shortages, Bernard Baruch urged the adoption of a forty-four hour week with no strikes or layoffs until January 1, 1949. General Motors' president, Charles E. Wilson advocated a forty-five hour work week as a brake on inflation. He estimated the current shortage of new cars and trucks at sixteen million vehicles.

Meanwhile shortages of pig iron, strip and sheet steel held down auto-mobile production and resulted in layoffs at a time when car demand was at record highs. On top of long postwar strikes in basic industries, passage of the Taft-Hartley law prompted 400,000 coal miners to take a ten-day holiday in June, causing additional cutbacks in steel production. Employes at Continental Motors also called the first sit-down strike in postwar years. It was to protest the disciplinary action taken against seventy-seven men for staging a "slow-down."

Automobile companies generally granted additional wage increases of fifteen cents an hour. Ford employes voted down a seven cents wage boost plus pension plan, in favor of a full fifteen cents an hour raise.

Businessmen who fancied making fortunes as new car dealers were attracted to Preston Tucker's rear-engine "Torpedo." Many poured money into his Chicago manufacturing venture.

Preston Tucker, leasing the huge Chicago plant where Dodge had made aircraft engines, unveiled a pilot model of his Torpedo to dealers in June. The Security & Exchange Commission, which had given his initial registration statement a glassy eye, now allowed him to proceed with the public sale of stock. California, however, banned the sale there a month later.

The Playboy Motor Car Company displayed a new lightweight automobile in New York, and Keller Motor Corporation introduced a Keller station wagon to a curious, milling audience at the Commodore Hotel. Davis Motorcar Co. showed off a three-wheeled vehicle in Los Angeles.

Packard, having commemorated the production of its one millionth car, became the first of the established manufacturers to introduce a complete new line of 1948 models.

Goodyear started production of a new "Super Cushion" tire, which it proclaimed the greatest improvement in the field since the introduction of the pneumatic tire in the early twenties. Seiberling brought out a heat-resisting casing it claimed was the "most nearly failure-proof" product since the war.

On the West Coast, the newly formed Davis Motorcar Co. glamorously demonstrated a three-wheeled motor vehicle, sought capital to build it.

Three automobile pioneers died in 1947: William Crapo Durant, founder of General Motors, William A. Brush, producer of the Brush "Runabout," and Henry Ford. Spring rains had flooded Ford's Dearborn, Michigan, estate, cutting off electric power. In April, America's "last billionaire" died by candlelight, with telephone communications shut off, in an atmosphere dramatically reminiscent of the world into which he was born.

The number of new car dealers in America had increased to 46,877, compared to 43,952 at the outbreak of the war, according to *Automotive News*. The Public Roads Administration placed the number of cars and trucks in use in the United States at 33,945,817 vehicles compared to 30,-638,429 in 1945. The typical passenger car owner in America's first full postwar year, 1946, used 651 gallons of gasoline and traveled 9,765 miles on the average, reported *The Detroit Times*.

In New York City, Mayor O'Dwyer eyeing the gasoline engine as a source of revenue, proposed a $5 levy on cars and $10 on trucks to be used for schools. Governor Dewey, needing funds to finance the soldiers' bonus, proposed a 1-cent a gallon tax on gasoline, and a $5 county and municipal tax on cars.

Chesapeake & Ohio railroad introduced an "auto ferry service," permitting train passengers to take their automobiles along on trips. Oldsmobile, whose Hydra-Matic drive eliminated the clutch pedal, announced that it had delivered 23,000 of its special Valiant models to disabled war veterans.

Despite a Boston banker's alarum that termination of credit restrictions would double the price of used cars, wartime controls over installment buying came to an end in November.

Tallying up at year-end, the automobile industry found it had enjoyed the highest sales of civilian production since 1937: 3,558,000 passenger cars and 1,240,000 motor trucks and buses had been built in U. S. plants for sale here and abroad, despite material shortages, price increases and production headaches.

The Jeepster, fancy version of the rugged military jeep, strutted from the Willys-Overland factory. This sports phaeton was mounted on a 104-inch wheelbase.   *Willys-Overland*

Economic Cooperation Administration

COLD WAR GENERALISSIMO

To direct the vast, multi-billion-dollar Marshall Plan aid to war-ravaged nations, the nation turned to an automotive man, Studebaker president Paul G. Hoffman. Western European nations made a swift economic recovery after the Economic Cooperation Administration began operating in 1948. With victory in sight on the economic front, ECA Administrator Hoffman made a final tour of inspection in Western Europe in 1950. From the Soviet-dominated sector of East Berlin, he restated his faith in the democratic processes emerging triumphant over the forces of compulsion. Outside the rubble of the old Reich Chancery, Mr. Hoffman pauses to converse with economist Howard Jones, adviser to ECA in Western Germany.

The lights and shadows that played across the American screen in 1948 reflected events and influences whose origins were deep-rooted in the recent past.

Economic forces generated by World War II, which had cost the United States financially $340 billion, continued dominant.

Inflation was being fought chiefly with "hold the line" statements from Washington, but the line sagged badly on all fronts, including the automotive.

Early in the year Studebaker president Paul G. Hoffman bluntly warned that new cars would be just as hard to get and would be no cheaper during 1948 and 1949. Executive vice president Ernest R. Breech indicated a "strong possibility" that new model Fords, due for June introduction, would be higher priced. Cost of making and shipping cars continued to mount. Steel prices were upped $6 a ton, railroad freight rates by 25 per cent. Launching a third round wage drive, the United Auto Workers formulated new wage demands for thirty cents an hour more. Coal and steel continued short, forcing suspension of operations in various motor plants. The new year was off to a start that greatly resembled its immediate predecessor.

The law of supply and demand began, however, to exert itself here and there. In March, the National Used Car Market Reports, Inc. announced that used car prices were about 10 per cent lower than in November, 1947. Prices of heavy trucks were shaved slightly. Several tire manufacturers lowered prices.

In a test case against a customer who disregarded a contract aimed at curbing new car resales, a Detroit dealer was awarded a $166 judgment. Several companies announced they were discontinuing fleet sales plans which had allowed large users of cars and trucks to purchase at a special discount. To protest an additional two cents gasoline tax increase, Louisiana service stations shut down entirely for one day.

The men and women who make automobiles continued to make news, too. Chrysler's plants were closed by strike for seventeen days. Pickets at Dodge heard Henry A. Wallace, candidate for president on the Progressive ticket, reiterate his previous statement that wages could be increased without price rises. Nearly the end of May, General Motors and the UAW-CIO reached a new type of wage agreement providing for an immediate increase of eleven cents an hour and a sliding wage scale geared to the cost of living. The U. S. Department of Labor stated that the agreement "may greatly influence the trend of collective bargaining in the United States." Chrysler and its workers, however, settled for a straight thirteen cents an hour wage increase. Studebaker, Packard and Ford did likewise, and others, including major parts suppliers, followed this pattern for the time being.

In early summer the consuming public heard the bad news. In terms of new prices it had to pay, the motorists' share of the increased wage, materials, and freight bills was to amount to $55 to $200 a car.

Seemingly, however, there was no end to the demand for passenger cars. Henry Ford II, reported that back orders for Ford, Lincoln and Mercury cars totaled more than 1,600,000. The National Automobile Dealers Association estimated the industry's unfilled orders for new cars at 7,300,000 up 11 per cent since January 1.

The American Iron and Steel Institute in June estimated a twenty million ton loss of raw steel because of strikes since the beginning of 1946. Before the month's end 230,000 General Motors and Ford workers were laid off for a week because of steel shortages. Parts shortages idled 15,000 more at Chrysler. Packard lines, lacking steel, went down soon after.

Customers, who hoped their name would reach the top of the waiting list in time to enjoy the summer's motoring, waited and waited and waited. One company blasted many such hopes by announcing it would be the middle of 1950 before the average car buyer could take immediate delivery of a new car.

Standard Oil of N.J.   An inhabitant of the metropolis commented on Manhattan's "bray of horns, the stink of exhaust fumes, and the crunch of crumpling metal . . ."

Then on the last day of summer, the Federal Reserve Board reinstated Regulation W, which placed controls on installment buying of new and used cars. By October, reports from all parts of the country indicated a resultant slide-off in used car prices. In November, Ford's J. R. Davis predicted a return to the buyers market within six months for cars selling above $2,500. Joseph Frazer of Kaiser-Frazer in December urged liberalization of Regulation W, warning that if allowed to stand it would "slow up the auto industry."

The size of the motor vehicle market appeared to be facing another limitation factor—traffic congestion. *Time* magazine provided a tart contemporary comment on the situation:

> In some big cities, vast traffic jams never really got untangled from dawn to midnight; the bray of horns, the stink of exhaust fumes, and the crunch of crumpling metal eddied up from them as insistently as the vaporous roar of Niagara . . .
>
> In Manhattan's garment district, where it often takes fifteen minutes to go a block through trucks, cabs and darting pushcarts, a taxi driver said: "we're beat. We got expressions just like people in Europe. It used to be you could get into a fight, but now even truck drivers take the attitude: 'If you wanna hit me, hit me'. They don't even get out to look at a fender . . ."
>
> But though postwar motorists were gradually becoming horn-blowing neurotics with tendencies toward drinking, cat-kicking and wife-beating, there were few who did not believe that the traffic evil would soon be corrected. This enormous delusion has been a part of U. S. folklore since the day of the linen duster, driving goggles and the high tonneau.
>
> Congress and state legislatures had appropriated millions to build super highways on which speeders could kill themselves at higher speeds. The traffic light, the yellow line, the parking lot, the parking meter, the underground garage, the one-way street, the motorcycle cop and the traffic ticket had all blossomed amid the monoxide fumes —and traffic had gone right on getting thicker and noisier year by year . . .
>
> Man steadfastly refused to see that nothing could solve the traffic evil but the fast-multiplying automobile itself. The problem would end for good on the day of the last traffic jam—at that shrieking moment when every highway, street, road and lane in the nation was so clogged with cars that none could ever move again . . . [1]

Money spent for road building and street improvement reached an all-time high—$3,000,000,000. More effort was being expended than ever before to teach youngsters how to drive; a growing number of high schools introduced training courses for the prospective motorist. An ego-deflating note to many an adult driver was sounded by Northwestern University Traffic Institute's director. He insisted that the poorest drivers in America

[1] *TIME*, December 15, 1947.

A.M.A.

Automotive leaders take time off from production problems to commemorate a production milestone—the making of the 100,000,000th motor vehicle in America.

were persons with very high or very low IQ's. The man who is "not too bright" is the safest, most careful of all drivers, director Ray Stannard Baker claimed, provided he "has good training, keen eyesight and is alert and fairly mature."

America's focus became increasingly directed in 1948 toward international problems. In mustering men to help out in the "cold war" being

Below, grouped at the speaker's table at the December 2, 1948, dinner were Chrysler's B. E. Hutchinson, Michigan Governor Kim Sigler, Secretary of Commerce Charles Sawyer, Nash-Kelvinator's George Mason, and Chrysler's K. T. Keller.

A.M.A.

waged, President Truman picked Paul G. Hoffman to become administrator of the Economic Cooperation Administration. Hoffman gave up his posts as head of Studebaker and of the Automotive Safety Foundation to direct the initial expenditure of $5.3 billion for European recovery. Shortage of dollars abroad was reflected in drastic import restrictions imposed on manufactured goods by various nations. Chief among the American products banned from entry abroad were American motor vehicles. United States exports declined to 442,000 cars and trucks, lowest level for a peacetime year since 1936.

Meanwhile, the pressing foreign demand for dollars, combined with a huge domestic desire for *any kind* of a new car, resulted in an unprecedented flow of foreign vehicles into the United States. In 1948, the import rate had climbed to 2,350 vehicles a month—a *monthly* rate in excess of the largest total imported in any previous year.

For the first time, the United Kingdom was sending more cars abroad than was the United States. American plants, however, were too busy trying to fill the demand at home to worry excessively. Viewed over a long-term basis, the record looked anything but discouraging. Over a half century, United States' motor vehicle production totaled 100,000,000 cars, trucks and buses, while the rest of the world combined was producing 24,000,000 motor vehicles.

The 100,000,000th American-made motor vehicle rolled off one of the industry's 112 assembly lines late in the week of August 13, 1948. Not until December 2, however, did the industry take time out formally to observe the event with a banquet in the Book-Cadillac Hotel in Detroit.

A commemorative booklet, *100 Million Motor Vehicles,* prepared by the Automobile Manufacturers Association for the occasion, pointed with pride to the production achievement and its economic consequences:

> Mass production of motor vehicles has helped give the United States a way of life far different from that in most nations.
>
> Traveling over our roads and streets in 1948 were more than 41 million motor vehicles—over six million more than in 1941. They were going about 400 billion miles a year, hauling more freight than all other transportation methods combined, and accounting for 85 per cent of passenger travel in this country.
>
> To serve these vehicles, we had surfaced more than half of our three million miles of rural roads, and most of our 300,000 miles of city streets. That gave us more surfaced routes than the rest of the world put together . . .
>
> Over 50 million people in the United States—one in every two persons over sixteen years old—were driving motor vehicles in 1948.

As an epitaph to its milestone year, the industry produced in its United States plants 5,285,000 motor vehicles, which exceeded all previous years' output, except for 1929.

NERVE CENTER OF DEFENSE

With the signing of the North Atlantic Treaty in 1949, in which twelve
nations pledged to put up a united defense against any Russian aggression,
activity stepped up at the Pentagon Building, located at Arlington, Virginia.
This aerial view of the building provides telltale evidence of big effort going
on inside—the parking lot is full.

ARRESTED DEVELOPMENT

How to keep the car driver from maiming, blinding, igniting, dazing, or bedazzling himself became a growing concern of legislators in 1949.

In thirty states, bills were introduced either prohibiting television in cars, or insisting they be so installed that the driver couldn't possibly sneak a look while caroming down the highway.

New Jersey banned the installation of self-service gasoline stations.

The U. S. Supreme Court held that advertising vehicles "constitute a distraction to vehicle drivers and pedestrians alike, and therefore affect the safety of the public in the use of the streets."

At a Highway Safety Conference in Washington, D. C., President Truman lambasted the sacrosanct State of Missouri where he said "even the insane" could get a driver's license for a quarter.

The buyer of motor securities also acquired a guardian or two. Preston T. Tucker got indicted on charge of mail fraud, conspiracy, and running afoul of the Security and Exchange Commission regulations. Later he was cleared of the charge. Playboy Motor Car Corporation was placed under Federal Court trusteeship pending reorganization. Ohio's security division refused to register a $5 stock issue of the Keller Motor Corporation.

Confidential street corner assurances that the "buyer's market is here at last" ran smack into a converse opinion from General Motor's president, C. E. Wilson. At GM's "Transportation Unlimited" exhibition in New York in January, he predicted that the 1949 car and truck market would reach the six million mark, and it would take at least another year to satisfy the demand of buyers.

But early in the year, the road ahead looked rocky for car salesmen. Jeremiahs sensed confirmation of their own gloomy predictions when in March the Federal Reserve Board relaxed installment buying controls, allowing twenty-one months for installment buyers to pay up instead of eighteen.

Several car companies reduced spring production schedules. Price cuts ranging from $12 to $270 on various makes were instituted. Ford's smallish English cars, the Anglia and Prefect, imported as a favor to dollar-hungry British, glutted the dealers' premises. But some American cars weren't moving very fast either.

Twice in the spring General Motors made wage reductions, amounting to three cents an hour in all, as result of its agreed-upon cost-of-living adjustment formula with employes. Each time, the company simultaneously announced price cuts on its cars and trucks.

Goodyear and Firestone reduced tire prices in the spring. Insurance companies lowered casualty rates on automobiles. It appeared that the peak of the postwar price spiral might have been reached.

Meanwhile, in early April, the United States and eleven other nations signed the North Atlantic Treaty, pledging to confront any Russian aggression with a united defense. The Berlin Blockade, which had stepped up the emotional tension of the "cold war," ended in May. In June, the United States Department of Defense began renewing its purchases of military motor equipment. Willys-Overland took on a contract for jeeps, Reo for trucks, and other automotive companies began producing parts for existing military models.

When General Motors permitted Ford to use its Hydra-Matic transmission in the Lincoln and Mercury, several other competitor companies scurried to President C. E. Wilson's office to seek similar arrangements. Meanwhile, Studebaker signed a contract with Borg-Warner for an automatic transmission, Buick stepped up production of its Dyna-Flow, and Packard got going on its Ultramatic.

Dodge, early in 1949, brought out a new roadster, giving the industry the first model under that designated name in fifteen years. Packard dealers drove home 1,500 gold-painted Golden Anniversary models, marking the company's half-century in business. Crosley put its "Hotshot," a two-passenger car, on display at Macy's Department Store. Studebaker's 1950 models sported an airplane fuselage-shaped hood. DeSoto unveiled a nine-passenger, four-door "Suburban." A modish model known as the "hard top convertible" emerged from several production lines.

In observing his eighty-fifth birthday in Lansing, R. E. Olds snorted that cars should be stripped of "too many gadgets" so they could sell for $1,000. A different viewpoint was expressed by Ford's J. R. Davis, who reminded customers that the price of the Ford included $379.78 in taxes, in addition to excise and other taxes on materials purchased by the manufacturer.

The fourth-round wage drive in 1949 was aimed at the steel industry, but it spilled over into Ford's negotiations. Ford management and unions signed a thirty-month contract featuring a $100-a-month company-financed pension plan. Goodyear ended a thirty-four-day strike a few days later by agreeing to a pension provision. Bethlehem Steel terminated its strike in a similar manner. Other major settlements followed. But the interrupted flow of materials caused by 1949 steel and coal strikes began to result in shut-downs in motor plants in the late fall. John L. Lewis ordered his striking soft coal miners to return to work until midnight November 30, as "an act of good faith designed to contribute to public convenience." Four rubber companies raised tire and tube prices 3.5 per cent. Steel companies increased their prices $4 or more a ton. The economic spiral began to nose upward once again, though car prices were not immediately affected.

Walter Reuther, Auto Union chief, signs pension agreement with Ford officials. John Bugas, labor relations vice-president, at right, is ready to sign for Ford management. Looking over Reuther's shoulder is William Clay Ford, youngest of Ford brothers.

Detroit News

During the year, Chevrolet reached another milestone in producing its 22 millionth motor vehicle. Cadillac achieved its first million unit off the line. The industry as a whole toppled over a previous all-time record for production, when on October 26 it surged beyond the mark set in 1929 for total vehicles made in one year. Output continued at a goodly pace, through the rest of the year.

On the record book it left a new high mark: 5,119,000 passenger cars and 1,134,000 motor trucks and buses produced in U. S. plants.

Robert L. Browning

DALLAS' DREAMWAY

Texas decided not to take its traffic headaches lying down. While bands played, Dallas in 1950 opened a stretch of its $12-million, 11-mile Central Expressway, which provided a six-lane freeway without a single stoplight. This new expressway shortened the cross-city journey by six miles, and in rush hours saved at least thirty minutes in motoring time. It carried three times as much traffic as an equal number of lanes on an ordinary highway.

RECORD BREAKER

Americans spent more for motoring in 1950 than their total outlay for doctors, dentists, religion, private education, life insurance, telephones, television, motion pictures, books, magazines and newspapers, Harry J. Klinger, a General Motors vice president observed.

New cars alone produced during the year could fill sixteen traffic lanes from Boston to Los Angeles, it was calculated. This output was likened by a pessimistic commentator, Lt. General Eugene Reybold, to a "flood threatening to inundate the country's outmoded highway system completely."

The Federal Reserve Board estimated that half the families in the nation now owned automobiles, and 4 per cent had more than one car. But, apparently, the industry had no intention of stopping at this point. From 1946 through 1950, auto manufacturers had invested $2 billion in new plants and tools to increase still further their capacity to produce.

The year commenced with the U. S. Department of Commerce forecasting a 10-20 per cent letup in sales. Studying his own sales projections, however, C. E. Wilson of General Motors optimistically predicted an industry market in 1950 of seven million passenger cars and one million motor trucks.

Actual production for the year came to the new all-time record of 6,666,000 passenger cars and 1,332,000 motor trucks from U. S. plants, while Canadian factories added 5 per cent more to the total.

The year saw the completion of the millionth postwar Studebaker, the 100,000th Willys-Overland station wagon, the millionth Oldsmobile with the Hydra-Matic drive, the 500,000th car from Kaiser-Frazer, and the 25,000,000th Chevrolet.

Business was so good for the British that they held an automobile show at Grand Central Palace to show off their wares. While continuing to shun their traditional exhibition site, American motor companies individually rented hotel lobbies, country clubs, town halls, and even football stadia to display their "new stuff."

Nash-Kelvinator in January invited guests to the Waldorf-Astoria, showed them a two-passenger light weight car, the "NXI," asked their opinion as to whether they'd buy it at $1,000 or less. Two months later, without waiting for similar advice, the company introduced a 100-inch wheelbase model, nostalgically named the "Rambler." In March, Crosley brought out a new two-seater "super sports model," priced for less than $1,000. Chevrolet introduced a new variant of the automatic transmission, the "Powerglide." Ford offered the "Fordomatic," and Mercury the "Merc-O-Matic." Packard took a busload of newsmen to a football stadium for a preview of its redesigned 1951 models, complete with "Ultramatic."

Kaiser-Frazer conducted a prize contest for a name for its new car, aimed for the popular-price field, selected the name "Henry J." This small-ish model made its debut in September, powered with "Supersonic" engines supplied by Willys-Overland. Hudson came along with a high-horse-power, higher-priced line, the "Hornet." Chrysler started production in the early fall on an all-steel "Town and Country" station wagon, followed three months later with a new line of Dodges, and early in 1951 made public a restyled group of passenger cars in all its lines.

Newcomers to the automotive sweepstakes, however, produced more lawyer's briefs and court writs than automobiles. Early in 1950 Tucker dealers filed reorganization plans with the defunct company's trustees, but eight months later decided it was impossible to proceed. A plan to revive the Playboy also got court approval, but then languished. Efforts to make the Davis three-wheel car ended in bankruptcy court.

Peace pacts with labor unions again had a prominent part in the industry's 1950 affairs. In May, General Motors signed a five-year peace agreement with the United Auto Workers. It provided for $125 maximum monthly pensions, increased insurance benefits and other features of a program which C. E. Wilson said was to "exploit machines, not men, and to share the bounty among employes, employers and customers."

Most car companies reduced prices in the late winter and spring. Station wagon prices were slashed as much as $250. The retail price structure was further shaken in the spring by a practice new to the postwar period; dealers in some areas turned a portion of their new products over to "unauthorized" merchandisers, who sold them at bargain prices. This practice was short-lived, however. International developments resulted in "scarcity" buying which gave a fillip to the new car business throughout the rest of the year. As wage and material costs proceeded upward, so too did car prices. The late fall saw prices going up again. The average retail price tag was $1,760, F.O.B., but before accessories and other extras.

A plug for automobile values emanated from a somewhat unexpected source, Federal Housing Expediter Tighe E. Woods. He pointed out that the 1950 model house cost three times more than the 1913 price for the same type of house; the 1950 eight-cylinder automobile, on the other hand, cost less than a one-cylinder car of 1903 vintage, he said.

In September, President Truman signed a bill calling for $500 million in Federal aid to highways over two years commencing in July, 1951. Earlier a Senate-House Economic Committee, headed by Senator O'Mahoney, placed the cost of putting the nation's highways and streets in shape at $41 billion. The year 1950 also marked the passing of John S. Haggerty, eighty-four-year-old, who built the first mile of concrete road in the nation, just north of Detroit's city limits, forty years before. Traffic problems continued to plague all cities. A few found sufficient funds to undertake expressway programs to alleviate the congestion.

In 1949, Nash invited opinions from the public as to the acceptability of its experimental model, known as the "NXI"—i.e. Nash Experimental International. (In 1954, the company brought out a refined version under the name Metropolitan.)

Dream roads, emerging from the drawing boards, were hailed as harbingers of the future. A forty thousand mile network, known as the Interstate Highway System, had been blueprinted in the late thirties. Now it was being translated, mile by mile, into hard multi-lane stretches known variously as expressways, skyways and freeways.

Breath-taking superhighways now cut straight through the heart of cities permitting the motorist to escape swiftly to the wide open spaces beyond. Starting its program two decades before, New York by 1950 had 400 miles of expressways crisscrossing, encircling and radiating from the world's biggest and busiest city. Detroit, while grinding out cars like sausages, built expressways at a snail's pace. Only two dozen miles of the motor city's projected 105 mile program were open to traffic. Told that at the current rate Detroit would still be pouring concrete in 1973 to complete its program, Mayor Albert Cobo prodded city officials into giving priority to expressway construction. Dallas, in characteristic Texan fashion, was meeting its congestion problem with a six-lane wonderway. It had opened a stretch of an eleven-mile ribbon of concrete that bisected Dallas, enabling traffic to speed from the heart of the city at forty-five miles an hour, twice as fast as on an ordinary city street. Los Angeles drivers skittered to the suburbs over the scenic Cahuenga Pass and Ramona Freeway. Fast a-building was the four-level Hollywood Freeway, spectacular example of a superhighway of the future.

PROBLEM IN SPACE AND TIME

The Korean crisis presented automotive production men with the problem of finding space, manpower and enough working hours to carry the twin load: defense and civilian output. New factories were built in the motor industry for specialized jobs. However, many companies made room in existing plants to accommodate various defense projects. This scene was taken at Chevrolet.

DUAL JOB

The easygoing American motorist, complacent in his belief that all's right with his world, received a jolt late one Sunday afternoon in June, 1950, when he turned on his car radio. A far-off, obscure, mountainous little land, North Korea, was giving us trouble.

As unfamiliar maps were projected on his television screen, he learned the whereabouts of the 38th parallel across which North Korean troops had slipped on the night of June 25. When President Truman ordered the United States Navy and Air Force to give "cover and support," John Q. Motorist, like millions of others, thought it would be only a matter of weeks before our South Korean friends were back in control of the situation.

But the car radio, day after day, gave off bad news. Russia's little crony, North Korea, was pushing us around.

The President asked for an extension of the Selective Service Act, for $10 billion to strengthen our armed forces, for businessmen to come to Washington to push production of war's hard metal goods. Actions reminiscent of other national emergencies again were imposed: restrictions of installment buying, ban on the fifth tire, control of car prices.

Again the defense agencies turned to Detroit for defense production. To handle the huge load, automotive companies constructed or converted more than forty plants for military production. In time more than 40 million square feet of additional floor space were added to the industry's facilities. But the problems of carrying a dual load in a dual economy were considerable.

Millions of Americans decided they couldn't postpone any longer the purchase of a new car, and factories worked double shifts supplying the demand. In tool rooms and engineering shops, technical men worked around the clock translating the defense orders into tooling requirements for the new military items. A Tank-Automotive center again was created in Detroit so that Army Ordnance could be nearer its biggest supplier, the automotive industry.

While Detroit, Flint, Toledo, South Bend, and Kenosha sweated out their defense assignments, another dramatic production effort was going forward in the one-time war plants of a recent enemy, Japan.

More than 60,000 weather-beaten combat vehicles were being resurrected from the jungles, the swamps, and the hills of Pacific islands, scattered from Guadalcanal to Okinawa. Abandoned when World War II ended, many of these trucks, tanks, jeeps, and other rolling stock were covered with tropical rot when the Korean War broke out. Hauled out of bogs with bulldozers, the equipment was brought to Japan by barge, completely dismantled, cleaned in oil baths, and assembled. Some 48,000 rebuilt units rolled off assembly lines in Yokohama and Tokyo nearly as good as new.

ROAD BREAK

First Marine Division rests on a Korean roadside after successfully overcoming an enemy ambush.

Rebuilding operations were carried on by native workmen in one-time Japanese arsenals and naval bases, using machine tools acquired under reparation payments, and supervised by American production experts.

The "ghost" equipment demonstrated its worth early. When American light tanks proved no match for the Russian tanks, the U. S. military officials drew upon its salvaged stock of thirty-two medium tanks to ship to Korea. From that initial start, a flow of trucks, half-tracks, ambulances, and other equipment moved forward to aid the UN troops, engaging first the North Koreans, then the Communist Chinese.

A group of Detroit automotive writers inspected these operations in the spring of 1952 and learned from the military authorities that the huge salvage program accounted for 84 per cent of the general-purpose vehicles used by the UN Army. Watching the equipment in action in Korea, one writer termed the Korean conflict a "second-hand war."

Back in America's mass production centers, however, spanking new equipment was being steadily built for the military. Fifteen motor vehicle companies were making military trucks. Automobile firms were working on eight different types of jet and turbo-prop aircraft engines. The Army spent $50 million in Michigan alone for ammunition in 1952, and proceeded to double the amount in 1953, spreading it over sixty-one Michigan companies with prime contracts.

President-elect Eisenhower, recognizing the automotive industry's importance in the defense economy turned to Michigan for his Secretary of Defense. Charles E. Wilson relinquished his job as president of General Motors and then accompanied his new "boss" on a trip to Korea. On his return home, he received his baptism of political fire over the question of whether he should retain his General Motors stock as Defense Secretary. On announcing his intention to sell, he was promptly confirmed for the post. Meanwhile, Roger Kyes left General Motors Truck to take on for a year the Number Two job in the Defense Department, Hugh Dean, a one-time Chevrolet production specialist, helped expedite the shell program, and Chrysler chairman, K. T. Keller, continued through most of 1953 to sparkplug the guided missile program, as he had for several years.

The automotive industry as a whole chewed up metal at a high rate through mid-year of 1953 as it produced tanks, cargo planes, marine engines, cannons, gun sights, rockets, guided missiles, and other items. With more than $6 billion in defense contracts on its books, the industry's defense production employment became substantial. Early in 1953 one out of five workers in Michigan's manufacturing industry was estimated to be on defense production. Contract cancellations followed the Korean Truce, however, which resulted in unemployment in defense centers.

OLD SOLDIERS NEVER DIE

As in the last war, the lowly jeep continued to carry the military great. Leaving for a tour of inspection of the front lines in February, 1951, were General of the Army Douglas MacArthur, at the time commander-in-chief, United Nations Command; in the rear Major General Doyle O. Hickey, acting chief of staff, GHQ; and between the two, Lt. General Matthew B. Ridgeway, who later in the year took over the Far East command when MacArthur was relieved of his command by President Truman.

U.S. Army Photo

Candidate Dwight Eisenhower in June, 1952, invades Motor Capital to seek pre-convention votes. The following month in Chicago, the Michigan delegation threw heavy Republican support behind the five-star general, helping pave the way for his nomination and election. Washington wits, noting the predominance of automotive people in his administration, punned: First came the New Dealers, then the Fair Dealers and now the auto dealers."

Designated as Secretary of Defense by President-elect Eisenhower, C. E. Wilson
announced to press that he'd resign his job as president of General Motors.
He later agreed to relinquish his company stock and other holdings.

RACY JOBS

After a lengthy period of mass-produced sameness in cars, revolt was inevitable. The urge for individuality resulted in a postwar rash of sport cars, foreign cars, home-built cars.

Mechanical devices to make driving effortless were sprouting steadily from research laboratories; yet, a cult of motorists turned to cars that called for skill and more personal participation in driving.

Romance began to be restored to motoring when road racing came back into vogue. The visual thrill once induced by the Stutz Bearcat and the Lincoln Continental was savored again as new styling was created. Many a father had lost touch with the mechanical intricacies under the hood of his latest model living-room-on-wheels; pater now blinked in ceaseless amazement at sons who rebuilt hot-rod cars from piles of old parts and coaxed their contraptions up to speeds in excess of 100 miles per hour.

As in the industry's early days, European styling trends exercised a strong influence on the American industry. Though small in numbers, the invasion of foreign cars was considerable in influence. Short wheel bases of some made parking easier. Their leather upholstery provided a touch of luxury. The simplicity and sauciness of the MG, for one, gave a low-budget driver a different car, with a snob appeal usually reserved for more costly models. For the more swank, the Jaguar provided for $4,000 great horsepower and distinctive lines. The ultra-ultra folk eyed, and some bought, French Delahayes and the Italian Ferraris with $15,000 price tags.

WHAT'S NEW

Crowds gathered wherever new cars were displayed. This Oklahoma City group has dropped into Chrysler's "New Worlds in Engineering" exhibit to hear about the new features, to visit with friends, to pick up the souvenir booklet and perhaps to acquire disturbing thoughts about how much longer the present family *Chrysler Corp.* jalopie can do service.

Packard Motor Co.

Designed to test public reaction to new styling, this Packard Panther sports car possesses a one-piece plastic body. The company exhibited the three-passenger model at auto shows, but announced no plans for putting it into production. A two-passenger sports convertible, below, the Buick Wildcat II was displayed at the GM Motorama as an experimental "dream car." The Wildcat has 100-inch wheelbase.

General Motors

The Dodge Firearrow, a product of the Italian school of experimental body design, stands only 46 inches from the ground to the top of its curved windshield. A sports roadster, the Firearrow combines the work of Chrysler stylists in Detroit and Ghia designers of Turin, Italy.

Nash noted the trend and put under contract Pinin Farina, Italian designer, who had won more than 100 Grand Prix for his custom styling and for contributions to the graceful lines of the Italian Fiat and Cisitalia, the French Renault, and the Jaguar. The Farina touch showed up in 1952 in the new styled Nash Ambassador and Statesman cars. For the select market willing to pay $5,000 for performance and individuality, the company served limited quantities of Nash-Healeys, a low-slung car, manufactured in three countries. The chassis came from Donald Healey in Warwick, England, the bodies were custom built in Farina's small Turin, Italy, factory, and major power components were made in Kenosha, Wisconsin.

In March, 1954, Nash brought out the 85-inch wheelbase, sporty Metropolitan, powered with a four-cylinder 42 horsepower Austin engine, equipped with a Fisher Ludlow Body, and built completely in England to Nash's specifications. The car gets 40 miles to the gallon and has a top speed of 70 m.p.h. Some 20,000 of these cars were ordered to test the American market for a stylish, but compact car. Price at the ports of entry was $1,469 for the convertible.

Chrysler turned to Italy for fine handicraft in body building. The company engaged the Ghia Company of Turin, a custom body builder, to translate a plaster model into a finished car, mounted on a Chrysler chassis, and powered with the Detroit-made 180 horsepower Firepower V-8 engine. The handbuilt model, known as the K-310, was shown publicly with Chrysler's regular 1952 line. Chrysler then followed with a succession of other Ghia idea cars, tagged with such names as the C-200, D'Elegance, Dodge Firearrow, DeSoto Adventurer and Plymouth Belmont, all blending

Nash Motors

Making a bid for the sports car market, Nash displayed at the 1951 Chicago Automobile Show its Nash-Healy, which measured only 38 inches from road to hood top. Major components of the car are made in three different countries. To capitalize on the appeal of European styling trends, Chrysler had an idea car, below, known as the K-310, designed in Italy and mounted on a Chrysler New Yorker chassis.

Chrysler Corp.

European styling with American engineering features. None were put into mass production.

Hudson Motor Car Co. also sought Italian styling skill, engaging Carrozzeria Touring of Milan, to turn out a sports car called the Italia. It stood nearly ten inches lower than standard Hudson models, and its rear fenders simulated jet stacks, which held tail, signal and back-up lights. No announced date was set for producing the experimental car in volume.

Packard brought forth a series of sporty experimental cars under the names of Pan American, Caribbean, Balboa and Panther. The Panther, powered with Packard's new 212 horsepower straight eight engine, was of one-piece plastic construction. No plans for producing the car for sale have been set.

Buick nodded to the sports car trend with a wire wheel production job called the Skylark, then followed with a 100-inch idea car called the Wildcat. Chevrolet's dream car, the plastic body Corvette, became a production model in mid-year, 1953, when it was given a $3,250 price and a 50-unit a month manufacturing schedule. Pontiac brought forth a 100-inch wheelbase experimental model, the Bonneville, which the driver enters by opening a hinged canopy of safety glass.

Kaiser joined the fibreglass body trend with a 36-inch high, rakish sports model known as the Kaiser Darrin 161 which was put on a limited production schedule. Factory price was set at $3,668.

Ford put on view early in 1954 a long, low steel body Thunderbird, equipped with a special composition hardtop, easily removable. While resembling a sports car, the Thunderbird is a two-passenger vehicle whose major parts are interchangeable with Ford's regular line of cars. The company announced it would be placed in production in the fall of 1954. Lincoln-Mercury displayed a four-passenger hardtop coupe, the XM-800. which it said could be produced if enough prospective customers asked for it. Riding the "dream" car trend with its competitors, Ford also unveiled the FX-Atmos, which translates as follows: FX stands for "future experimental," and Atmos, which "has been taken from the 'atmosphere' and connotes free and unlimited creative thinking." The company announced that the 48-inch high, 221-inch long vehicle "is not proposed as a future production vehicle, and for that reason, no engineering considerations have been involved in its development."

The industry's growing tendency to show off its idea cars was a complete reversal of its pre-war policy, which called for closely guarding the dream children being nurtured in engineering laboratories and styling sections. But the new policy had its roots in sound merchandising concepts, for the public flocked around the futuristic and fantastic models and many motorists lingered long enough to become interested in a model of current vintage more suitable to the purse.

LOVE AND DEVOTION

Tenderness and care comprise the home-car designer's approach to his work. With infinite patience and skill, he slaves lovingly over his creation, getting the exact sweep to his fender lines and the proper gloss to the surface finish. The sports car *afecionado* above is sanding down the body after its fourth coat of lacquer. Two more coats are yet to come. While the finished product may bear scant resemblance to a mass-produced Detroit car, some of the elements of Detroit are there. Grill and headlights of this home-workshop masterpiece come from the 1951 Ford.

Millionaire sportsman Briggs S. Cunningham built a small business in catering to the vogue. By fashioning his own bodies for Chrysler and Cadillac power plants, and adding other standard Detroit components, he attracted a following in the $9,000-a-car price class. Such efforts were emulated by others of a creative bent, who in their own workshops slaved over hood and fender lines to bring out something exciting, exotic, and individual. A new group of magazines for the race car devotee featured articles on "Customize It Yourself," "Tune It On the Dynamometer," "Overhauling the MG Engine," and invited the use of question-and-answer columns where the home mechanics could discuss their problems and triumphs. The league of sports car builders straddled those who could afford as much as $10,000 in rebuilding their cars down to those operating on a financial shoestring and using parts from depression vintage cars, or earlier. Their common bond was the love of taut steering, which made driving a skillful art, and of powerful engines that responded vigorously to the toe touching the accelerator.

The sports car specialist found pleasure in baiting the motor car factories, and in nose-thumbing at Detroit's efforts to modify regular production vehicles in an attempt to give them a sports car touch. A spokesman for the group, John G. Kingdon, wrote:

"Just for the record, we'd like to tell them (Detroit stylists and sales officials) exactly what a sports car is and isn't.

"First of all, it *isn't* a mile-long, poorly balanced, dipped-in-chrome gook wagon. It has few automatic gadgets. Potential sports-car owners want to be *drivers,* not operators; they want to *exert control* rather than to have nearly everything done automatically for them. They *don't* want power steering, power brakes, or automatic transmission.

"OK, so now we know what features a sports car *doesn't* have; but what exactly *does* it have? That's easy; it has rapid acceleration, high top speed, and the ability to maneuver at fast speeds in close quarters, around corners and over hilly terrain."*

It was claimed that the United States boasted 500,000 hot rod enthusiasts among its motorist population. After a period of having a rough time at the hands of the legal authorities who thought them "speed maniacs," the young experimentalists began to gain respectability and persuaded police departments to close normal highways for their periodic events. The more ardent groups raised funds for their own "drag-strip," on which to test their lowered center of gravity vehicles. No hot rod was typical, but a representative one might consist of 1932 Ford fenders, 1934 Chevrolet headlights, 1948 Oldsmobile bumpers, a modified Mercury engine, a re-worked Auburn instrument panel, and upholstered bucket seats from an English Austin. The outside of the car might well be Indian Ceramic (reddish-pink) and the interior chartreuse and black leather upholstery. The conversation of the hot rodder was sprinkled liberally with reference to dual carburetors, piston displacement, gear ratios, tappet clearance, and overlap. Their mecca was the Bonneville, Utah, salt flats, where a racer using straight alcohol for fuel could attain speeds of 153 m.p.h. and could reach 145 m.p.h. on gasoline.

Other sports car lovers flocked to Watkins Glen, N. Y., for races over hill and dale, to picturesque Elkhart Lake, Wis., or to the closed course route at Bridgehampton, N. Y. In an atmosphere of super-charged excitement, 35,000 or more spectators lined the courses to watch the Jaguars, Allards, Ferraris, and Cunninghams take the right angle turns and the high speed curves. As in the early Vanderbilt race, crowd control was not too good at times, with unlucky spectators getting in the path of racers.

Organizations such as the Sports Car Club of America, which had grown from a handful of enthusiasts to more than 2,500 members in post-war years, laid down the rules and sponsored these colorful road races. They insisted that, unlike the straight racing car, the sports car must be equipped with headlights, self-starter, hand-and-foot brakes, and other standard units used in regular highway driving.

*From *Sports Cars and Hot Rods,* December, 1953.

The National Association for Stock Car Auto Racing provided competitive meets for drivers who were unable to afford the big-time, $25,000 race car of the type used at the Indianapolis Speedway races. Piston and bearing clearances on standard cars were opened up to give a freer running engine and added horsepower. The spark was also advanced, and richer carburetor jets were often used. The Hudson Hornet, Oldsmobile '88, Plymouth, and other makes competed for points on NASCAR's Grand National Circuit. Tim Flock of Hapeville, Georgia, copped top honors in 1952's season. Herb Thomas, driving a Hudson Hornet, won twelve starts in the 1953 event, beating the previous record of nine winning starts.

Marshall Teague, a Daytona Beach driver, piloted Hudson cars to set eighteen out of twenty-nine track records recognized by the American Automobile Association in races on its stock car circuit. He became the 1952 AAA title winner, as well as the holder of nine of eleven national marks in these contests. In 1953, Frank Mundy, the "Atlanta Rebel," took top honors.

Stock-car racing drew sizable post-war crowds. Shown above is the Langhorne, Pennsylvania dirt track with Dick Rathman, the ultimate winner, already leading the May 4, 1952 race at the beginning of the second lap. The event was 150 miles long.

Hudson Motor Co.

Driver George Hammond, winner of the Pike's Peak climb in 1952, shows car owner Leo Dobry his good-luck charms. These baby booties of the driver's granddaughter are usually worn in Hammond's helmet when the race is on.

Speed Age Magazine

American cars competed, too, outside the country in the grueling twenty-four hour race at LeMans, France. A Nash-Healey finished third in 1952, with top honors taken by two German Mercedes. The tortuous 1,912 mile Pan American Road Race from border to border in Mexico found 1953 Lincoln cars sweeping to the first four places in the unlimited stock car class.

Pikes Peak continued to challenge the stamina of men and cars. In 1952 the annual Pikes Peak Hill Climb was won by George Hammond, a forty-nine-year-old Colorado Springs grandfather, who wore a pair of baby shoes in his helmet and timed his own pace with a stop watch pinned to his sweatshirt. Driving a 270 Offenhauser up the mountain course, where fog often limited visibility to thirty feet, Hammond reached the top in fifteen and a half minutes. This was just two seconds short of the all-time mark set in 1946 by Louis Unser, known as "the Old Man of the Mountain." Unser regained top laurels in 1953, when he drove to victory a Federal Engineering Special.

A new historical status was bestowed on the sport of speeding when the Automobile Racing's Hall of Fame was established in 1953. Ten men were selected to have their likenesses and chronicles of their deeds enshrined in a special exhibit at Ford's Greenfield Village, near Detroit.

Henry Ford, driver and inventor, made the list. Others included Barney Oldfield, first man in America to drive a mile-a-minute; Ray Harroun, who won the first 500 mile race in Indianapolis; Louis Chevrolet, world famed figure on dirt tracks and speedways; William K. Vanderbilt, sponsor of the Vanderbilt Cup Races; Bert Dingley, a national race champion in 1909 and a leading contender earlier; Carl Fisher, father of the Indianapolis Speedway; Harvey Firestone, whose tires were on many winning race cars; T. E. (Pop) Myers, who served as a member of the Speedway management from 1910 to 1953; Fred Wagner, famous starter, who originated the present system of flagging races.

In 1954, four more names were added: Eddie Rickenbacker, the speedway daredevil who became an airlines executive; Ralph DePalma, considered by some the greatest driver developed in America; Earl Cooper, who drove the Stutz to fame, and Ralph Mulford, who dominated road racing prior to World War I.

A variety of organizations, whose members shared a mutual affection for motor vehicles, old or new, held meets or meetings galore. Among the most prominent was the Veterans Car Club of America. One serious-minded group assembled under the name of Auto Maniacs of America. Still another, affluent enough to support permanent headquarters on Manhattan's Madison Avenue, was the Automobile Old-Timers, which made a full-time business of promoting motordom's "good old days."

STEAM UP

This old photograph of the Stanley Steamer's successful climb in 1906 provides a colorful reminder that this precipitous climb is no recent feat. As early as 1899, Francis E. Stanley and his wife had climbed Mount Washington in two hours in one of their Steamers.

Brown Bros.

GANGWAY

The difference between a seller's market and a buyer's market, an old automotive axiom holds, is "one carload of cars". Sometime in the summer of 1953 that last carload arrived, and the scramble for customers was on in earnest.

For the first time in more than a dozen years, the customer figuratively was back in the driver's seat, insofar as merchandising relationships were concerned. He again was in position to haggle over new car prices, jockey for a good deal on his trade-in, and walk away to try for a better buy elsewhere.

The car market had held firm longer than most industry observers had dared to predict. An all-time record production was established in 1950 when 6.6 million units were made. Then under governmental restrictions production had fallen off to 5.3 million in 1951 and 4.3 million in 1952. During the first half of 1953, new passenger car production records were set, followed by a slide-off in sales in the second half. Even so, the passenger car total reached 6.1 million units, the second best year in history.

But a pronounced shift in the market was in the making early in the year. Government controls were lifted, credit terms for customers were eased, steel became readily available for production. Slam-bang competition came back with a vengeance.

Indianapolis Motor Speedway

On the company's 50th anniversary, Ford furnished the pace car for the Indianapolis Motor Speedway. William Clay Ford grins at Speedway president Wilbur Shaw, who rode with him on the pace lap of the 1953 race. Dodge provided the pace car for the 1954 event.

Nash made a spirited bid for the station-wagon market. In its Rambler Cross Country, the manufacturer lengthened the Rambler's wheelbase to 108 inches, incorporated Pinin Farina styling and installed an auxiliary luggage carrier on the roof.

Some real issues were ripe for settlement in the market place. Big cars vs. light-weight ones. Medium vs. low-priced vehicles. Custom vs. stripped-down jobs. American vs. foreign cars. Detroit vs. Continental styling. Steel vs. plastic bodies.

The turn in the market arrived at varying times for different dealers and different makes. By fall of 1953 it had arrived for all.

Discount selling of new cars became widespread. Under the impact, the used car market broke. The average wholesale price declined from $944 to $710 during the year—a drop of nearly 25%.

For a brief period, a few frenetic dealers indulged in "blitz" selling. Dealers motivated salesmen with promises of premium commissions, and staged community razzle-dazzles to pull in the customers. Sales of 100 or more cars in a single day were recorded by single dealerships, but the "blitz" was short-lived on the American automotive scene.

Dealer advertising beseeched customers to "Come in and write your own deals." Salesmen were promised all-expenses-paid trips to Havana, Hawaii and Paris in sales contests sponsored by factories and dealers. As in days of shortages, new cars appeared on used car lots—but at bargain prices. The practice was termed "car bootlegging", which meant that some new car dealers were unloading heavy inventories of cars on used car merchants at prices below retail levels.

With competition tough, car makers expanded their 1954 lines, stepped up their horsepower, lengthened their car bodies, added more optional equipment. *Automotive News* reported: "In their quest for buyers, auto firms apparently felt it was necessary to jazz up their offerings to a higher degree than originally planned."

A trend was well underway toward such deluxe features as air conditioning, power steering, power brakes, plastic tops, raise-or-tilt front seats, squeal-proof tires.

All but three of the score of cars introduced early in 1954 had higher horsepower ratings. Chrysler, whose V-8 is rated 235 horsepower, nosed out the previous year's leader, Cadillac, which boasted a 230-horsepower engine. Three companies were expected to introduce cars with at least 260 horsepower engines within the 1955 model year. Reports from Society of Automotive Engineers meetings in June, 1954 indicated that passenger cars with 400 horsepower ultimately will appear. An entirely new principle in automatic transmission was anticipated on one 1955 model. Further elimination of the rigid steel frame, which supports the under body of the car, also was predicted in some quarters. Nash, Hudson and Willys already had frameless construction, and a Big Three producer was reported ready to adopt this principle, which is widely used in cars made abroad.

Late in 1953 eight-cylinder cars outsold six-cylinder models for the first time. In the first postwar year, 1946, sixes had outsold eights by a margin

Studebaker Corp.

Raymond Loewy, designer of the 1953 Studebaker, fondles his newest baby at the company proving ground near South Bend, Indiana. The 101-year-old company spent $27 million to change over to the new model, which created considerable attention when introduced, just as had Loewy's 1947 creation, the "two-way" Studebaker.

201

General Motors

Chevrolet found public reaction so gratifying to its experimental Corvette that in 1953 it put the glass-fiber reinforced plastic model into limited production and offered it at a list price of $3,250.

of 88.4%. But in the 1953 model year, there were 21 models on the market with eight cylinders and 18 with six cylinders. Of the eights, 15 had V-type engines, six had straight-eight engines.

Automobile shows were staged to show off the products and stimulate customer interest. The National Automobile Show, dormant since 1940, continued to stay in mothballs. Detroit dealers, however, staged a highly patronized exhibition, as did Chicago, Dallas, Los Angeles and many other cities.

General Motors moved into the Waldorf-Astoria annually to show off its products, present and future, in elegant surroundings, replete with music, ballet and moving double-deck stages. The exhibit, known as the Motorama, then was packed off to Miami, Los Angeles and San Francisco for repeat performances. Feature of the 1954 Motorama was a gas turbine automobile, built only for proving ground and test track, not for the public highways. Hot compressed gas was funneled through a power turbine directly connected via a two-speed transmission with the car's rear wheels to power the vehicle. The power plant has a weight-to-power ratio of approximately two pounds per horsepower, which is about one-third the ratio of a conventional piston engine and drive. The single seater experimental vehicle with aerodynamic styling was named the XP-21 Firebird.

Chrysler Corporation, too, barnstormed around the country with its line of new products, including a spate of experimental vehicles. Chrysler also, developed a gas turbine and fit it into a standard Plymouth.

Fire effected some important changes in General Motor's plans in the months preceding the introduction of its 1954 models. In August, 1953, oil-fed flames ravaged GM's Hydra-Matic plant, stopping production on the automatic shifting units for three months, forcing Cadillac and Oldsmobile to install the Dynaflow drive and requiring Pontiac to use the Powerglide transmission.

Sparks flew, too, in the traditional rivalry, Ford vs. Chevrolet. Ford set a hot pace in the latter half of 1953, but Chevrolet again emerged in first place for the year as a whole in production and registration totals. In the early months of 1954 Ford pushed into the lead by a slight margin.

Young Bill Ford, becoming more prominent in the triumvirate of Ford brothers, assumed a pacemaker's role at the May 30, 1953 Indianapolis Speedway race. He drove a Ford car on the pace lap in a race won by Bill Vukovich of Fresno, California. Dodge furnished the pace car for the 1954 race. Vukovich won again, averaging 130 m.p.h.

The independent car companies, giving pitched battle to the Big Three —General Motors, Ford and Chrysler—made preparations for even more intense competition. Nash-Kelvinator and Hudson agreed to consolidate, and to assemble both cars in Nash's plants in Wisconsin. The new $335,-000,000 combination, named American Motors Corporation, became one of the largest manufacturing organizations.

Not only did General Motors emphasize continental styling, but they nabbed a continental celebrity, the Duke of Windsor, for photo-taking purposes at their Motorama. To his right are chairman Alfred P. Sloan and scientist C. F. Kettering. The experimental convertible contained a 250-h. p. Cadillac engine.

General Motors

General Motors

Tokyo raider General James Doolittle, right, shares the front seat of Cadillac's "Le Mans" experimental car with Major Alexander P. De Seversky, the aircraft designer, and Mrs. De Seversky. Cadillac's J. M. Roche has his back to an artist's visualization of the Le Mans 24-hour race. A custom-built Chrysler phaeton, below, with a concealed tonneau top provided a touch of swank reminiscent of the Pierce-Arrow of two decades ago. Driving is made easier for the chauffeur by power steering.

Chrysler Corp.

In 1953, Kaiser-Frazer and Willys also merged, marketing their cars under the name of Kaiser-Willys. In the motor truck field, White and Autocar, two of the oldest commercial vehicle producers, decided to face the future together under one management. Crosley, which earlier had dropped from the automobile industry, merged with Aerojet Engineering Corporation. Chrysler purchased Briggs, veteran builder of automobile bodies. Packard President James J. Nance who had expressed a desire to make his company an "attractive bride" for a merger found a willing partner in Studebaker. On June 22, directors agreed to merge the two companies, subject to ratification by stock-holders later in the year.

Some notable milestones were chalked up in 1953. Plymouth produced its eight millionth car, Chevrolet turned out its 30 millionth, and Ford in the year of its 50th anniversary rolled the 40 millionth car off the final assembly line. Buick, too, celebrated its Golden Jubilee in 1953.

No one seemed to agree just how big the total market for cars would be in the United States. The President's Material Policy Commission in a 1952 report had come up with a prediction for 1975. The Commission said:

"At the beginning of 1950 there was in use in the United States 1 car for about every 3 persons 14 years of age or over. By 1975 there is expected to be 1 car to every 2½ persons over 13, or around 65 million cars*!"

Another prognosticator, C. K. Glaze, Chairman of the Third Annual Highway Planning Conference, boldly declared that in the year 2034, "There'll be more cars than people."

With the streets and highways already congested, some users of motor vehicles shuddered at the thought of still more cars and trucks competing for the available space. Highways were still wearing out faster than new ones could be built.

The property damage in a single year by motor vehicle accidents was placed at $1.4 billion by the National Safety Council. With more than 1,000,000 people killed to date in automobile accidents, the press and pulpit took after the motor car with renewed zeal. One Sunday in 1953, as part of a highway safety program, 500 Vermont clergymen delivered similar sermons stressing the commandment "Thou Shall Not Kill." ICC Commissioner James K. Knudson a few days later complained in Detroit that there were "too many 100-mile-an-hour cars being operated on 50-to-70 mile-an-hour roads." Harvey Firestone, Jr. estimated it would require $5 billion to $7 billion a year for the next fifteen years to meet the nation's highway needs.

Yet, progress was being made. Private cars were estimated to be carrying 85 per cent of the nation's combined local and long-distance traffic.

*From *Resources for Freedom*, Volume II, the Outlook for Key Commodities, A Report to the President by the President's Material Policy Commission.

Metropolitan communities were pushing expressway construction. Twenty-eight states were building super highways. Private capital was being invested in turnpikes and toll roads. Traffic safety measures and better traffic control methods were being instituted throughout the land. (New Jersey installed lane dividers that "talked" to the motorist if he strayed too far from his side of the road.)

Driving was being made easier for the motorist. Power steering was offered on many American makes. Nearly half of all passenger cars being built contained automatic transmissions. More than nine out of ten postwar cars were equipped with car radios.

Motels outnumbered hotels two to one. 37,000 cars were operated by rental services. The Federal Tax Collector was taking in $2 billion annually in automotive excise taxes.

The petroleum industry claimed that the American motorist's gasoline was giving him performance that was 67% improved over that of 25 years ago. And L. S. Wescoat, President of the Pure Oil Company, declared that today's automobile, based on useful life, was 72% cheaper than its 1925 counterpart.

Lincoln-Mercury

"Not a 'dream car,'" maintains Lincoln-Mercury, but one that can readily be produced if the public desires an ultra-modern mechanism. Bearing the cryptic designation of XM-800, this four-passenger hardtop coupe was displayed at automotive exhibitions across the nation in 1954.

Be that as it may, the automobile, indeed, seemed here to stay. Its stay seemed assured because its user had developed a special kind of attachment for his product. *Fortune* magazine viewed it thusly:

"The most important single fact about cars," said the magazine, "is the fact that Americans love them. Never has an industry produced a machine that has so inflamed the proprietary instinct in so many prospects; never has an industry's output gratified both the senses and the psyches of so many customers."

Fortune classified the average American car owner as *a rolling potentate* who "takes immense pleasure merely in polishing it and tuning it up, or simply contemplating it. And who can chide him? Where and when, as a matter of fact, has the world produced so happy a union of mechanical excellence, sheer elegance, and low cost*?"

Warming up to the subject, *Fortune* continued: "As the advertising writers put it, accurately enough, his car responds to his every whim—something nothing or nobody else does. It lets up exactly when he wants it to, and lays on exactly when he wants it to. It enables him to rush forward and leave other things and other people behind—to assert himself successfully. He is not really annoyed by the time and anger he expends in genealogical exchanges with jokers who try to push him off the road or try to prevent him from pushing them off. On the contrary, these encounters enable him to vent a whole week's accumulated anger and frustration, and in a way he never can at home or work. The car is fulfillment—and fulfillment of a kind never before vouchsafed to so many people."

* From *Fortune*, September, 1953.

An experiment in reinforced fibreglass construction, the Plymouth Belmont, was designed as a sports car on a standard chassis. The seats are individual bucket type upholstered in white leather.

Plymouth

Chrysler Corp.

An all-plastic body mounted on a 114-inch Dodge chassis made its debut early in 1954 under the name of the Granada. It is an experimental car.

Ford Motor Co.

Henry Ford II fondles the all-steel Thunderbird, whose overall height of 51.5 inches makes it nearly a foot lower than the 1954 Ford sedan. The Thunderbird's top is removable.

Willys Motors

In production at Willys Motors is the Kaiser Darrin 161, a fibreglass sports car, 36 inches high and 15 feet long. Among the car's features are sliding doors which move into the front fenders when in open position. The University of Michigan football stadium at Ann Arbor provides the setting for this photograph.

Hudson Motor Co.

The Hudson Italia, an experimental car, is 10 inches lower than the standard Hudson models. The body was designed in Milan, Italy, by Carrozzeria Touring.

Willys-Overland

After concentrating on jeep production through early post-war years, Willys brought out its first passenger sedan in its Golden Aniversary year, 1952. Here's the 1953 model Willys.

Nash Motors

Bucking a trend toward bigger cars, Nash bet millions that the public would accept a compact car with style. Added safety is afforded passengers in this convertible through steel side rails.

General Motors

NO BUSINESS LIKE SHOW BUSINESS

As the industry entered a period of intense merchandising, show business again became an important part of the auto business. For seven days each January at the Waldorf-Astoria, General Motors put on its lavish Motorama, where current models and "dream" cars were displayed at their elegant best. To choral crescendos, orchestral overtones and ballet gyrations a pageant of cars moved automatically on and off a revolving stage. In the left foreground is GM's gas-turbine car, called the Firebird, a stellar attraction at the 1954 Motorama. Just as forty years earlier, automobile parades, below, usually produce a good turn-out in Western towns. These gaily decorated vehicles, participating in the opening of the 14th annual Rodeo at Elk City, Oklahoma, represented Nash's American-made line — Rambler, Statesman and Ambassador.

Nash Motors

Most expensive fire in automotive history occurred on August 12, 1953 when the
Detroit Transmission Division of General Motors was swept with flames which
halted production of automatic transmissions used on Cadillac, Oldsmobile,
Pontiac, Lincoln, Mercury, Nash, Kaiser and Hudson. The fire accounted for
$50 million in damages, caused General Motors to seek other facilities for trans-
mission production. The company at first leased a portion of the near-by Willow
Run plant, then bought the plant for $26 million.

O, DO YOU REMEMBER

Main Street's never been quite the same since America hitched its destiny to automotive transportation. Whether to escape life's monotony or to keep up with the Joneses, Americans have found that the automobile is one of life's necessities. While most people cuss at the problems it created, few want to go back to the kind of economy that existed before the first horseless carriage disturbed Main Street's slumbers.

Culver Service

Did the automatic transmission slip, the electric window lift stick, the automatic choke fail to function? Hold your temper, brother! Glance back down the road, and you'll realize how far you've come. At least your neighbor doesn't allow as how "the durned thing ain't never gonna work."

Philip Gendreau

AVERAGE MOTORIST IN MOTION

Here, perhaps, is the typical American motorist. He's behind the wheel every day and usually drives more often than wife or daughter. He picked up this car secondhand, paid for it on the installment plan, and will roll up another 9,500 miles on it this year. The car is six and a half years old now; so he'll sell it in another year or two, and buy another one with less mileage on the odometer. The car above meanwhile, will pass on to several other owners before it finally is junked. However, its functional parts will be melted down to make more steel to make more automobiles. But the typical driver above isn't worrying too much about that. He finds "the old bus" plenty good enough to get him to-and-from work, to run his wife downtown or to the store on Saturdays, and for the family to have some fun together over the week end. Like most statistical concepts, however, this driver won't remain typical very long. Before he rounds the bend, he'll be succeeded by a new model "average motorist" who'll probably resent being called "average" if you dare try.

If tomorrow's traffic moves on more highways like the above, shown outside San Diego, motorists will save countless millions of dollars in time, gasoline consumption and lower accident costs.

218

Postscript

TOMORROW'S PROMISE

Americans characteristically look with boundless enthusiasm to the future. A transportation-minded people, they own 75 per cent of the world's automobiles. In the next quarter century, they hope to build, use and discard another 125,000,000 motor vehicles.

Already nearly seven out of ten American households have a car. One out of twelve boasts two or more motor vehicles. The American farmer has long outgrown his hostility to the automobile; cars now outnumber bathtubs and telephones on farms.

The automobile, in fact, constitutes the biggest single item, except for food, in the budget of the *homo sapiens Americanus.*

The motor car makers keep designers and engineers busy on something new, something different, something better. Used-car dealers, too, are joining the parade; they now can spray a liquid product into well-worn interiors that produces "new car aroma." Progress continues, in one form or another.

"BIRD" IN FLIGHT

First gas-turbine automobile built in the United States, General Motors' XP-21 Firebird skims over a test track outside Phoenix, Arizona. The Firebird incorporates aircraft styling, using a vertical tail fin and swept-back wings on its glass fiber-plastic body. It was constructed to test the gas turbine's possibilities for ground vehicles and characteristics of aerodynamic design. At the wheel is test driver Mauri Rose, veteran of the Indianapolis Speedway, who is afforded protection by a plastic-covered cockpit.

General Motors

Buick Motor Div.

Buick's XP-300, capable of 150-m.p.h. speed, is another car built for experimental engineering purposes. Out of such tests may emerge the cars of tomorrow. This particular car, Ford's FX-Atmos, below, never will go on sale, but it may well influence the styling concepts of millions of passenger cars to be built in years to come. This model is 48 inches high, 80 inches wide and 221 inches long.

In the period immediately ahead, air conditioning promises to maintain car interiors at constant temperatures in summer or winter. Within a decade, say some, more cars than homes will have air conditioning, as the price of present expensive systems plummet.

Car seats already can be made into beds, and electric shavers are available to operate on the car battery. Truck-trailers are planned that will be convertible into a 14 by 20 foot room. Cars of tomorrow are expected to carry food warmers and coolers. If the trend continues, a family need never go home.

Aircraft developments seem likely to find their way into automobile construction. Electrically heated windshields and window glass are being considered for cars. Sanding devices, such as are used on locomotives, are already offered winter drivers for quick starting and stopping on icy pavements.

Better engines and fuels have combined in the past two decades to produce a 40 per cent increase in top speed, 46 per cent in fuel economy and 60 per cent in horsepower, while limiting car weight to a 7 per cent increase. Engineers predict a continued increase in fuel economy. An additional increase of 30 per cent is foreseen, which would result in a $2.5 billion annual savings in American motorists' gasoline bills.

Here's how your car might look if it had a drop nose and suspended parking light. From such designs, few completely new cars evolve. But from time to time an interesting feature so envisioned leaps from the sketch pad into the hard reality of production.

Kaiser-Willys

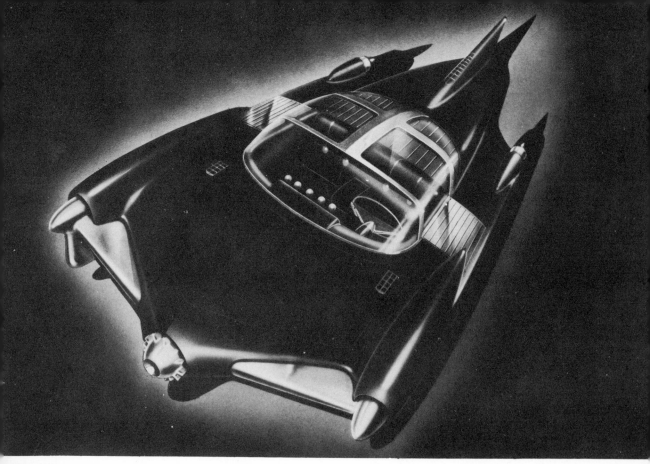

Kaiser-Willys

The tail fin, which started out as a protruding rear fender, completes its evolutionary cycle in this front-wheel drive, three-wheel vision of the future depicted by a Kaiser stylist.

New materials are on the horizon, which will make automobiles lighter and more sturdy. Light metals and plastics are making inroads on steel. Indicative of a trend is the fact that today's car already contains 260 different chemical products. Abundant in the earth's crust is titanium, which contains many of steel's physical properties, yet weighs only half as much. Although now prohibitively high in price, it's a good bet for tomorrow's cars. In the ocean there is an inexhaustible supply of magnesium, for which greater use is seen in the automobile industry. Glass-fibre reinforced plastics will be subject to increased experimentation and use. Sheet and cast aluminum, which also holds low-weight advantages, will loom prominently in automotive thinking.

Car designers, their imaginations racing ahead of advancing technologies, will continue to project their thinking into unorthodox realms of styling and design. In their styling sections are air-brushed renditions of three-wheeled cars, rear-engined jobs, vehicles with extreme fins and some with wings. They have in process clay models of cars with shorter wheel bases, some with longer; some bodies that are narrower, some wider. Whether their dreams, sketches, and mud versions materialize into actual cars depends on many things. Not the least is this factor: will the customer buy it?

Not all the effort, of course, will go into revolutionary concepts of transportation. Some earnest thinking will be directed at motordom's frill segment. Conscious that the customer has always decorated his car with fancy radiator ornaments, fox tails, sun visors, geegaws and knickknacks, the accessory makers have little cause for gloom as they scan the future for sales features. This phase of human foibles was philosophically presented by a motorist in a letter to a car manufacturer:

> A man is accused of being a cad if he boasts of his love affairs. He is called an inflamed egotist if he should say a few words about himself. His natural pride in his children may be construed as boring bragging. Thus, his automobile becomes the safety valve for pride. In it he discovers all the hidden virtues lacking in a normal frustrating existence. So give him all the gadgets you can. They are his toys. Aside from giving him comforts and luxuries his own home may not possess, they give him something to talk about.

The vagaries of the American motorist's taste will be determined only by tomorrow. And the methods of supplying him with personal transportation will be greatly changed by new technologies. But the question of how effectively he will be able to use his cars remains highly debatable. But here, too, optimists can be found.

Harvey Firestone, Jr., predicts that 62,000,000 motor vehicles will roll over the nation's highways in 1960. With every new vehicle that takes to the highway, he warns, the entire automotive system moves "inch by inch nearer paralysis." However, the progress in the past, he told an American Automobile Association audience, indicates that the nation is on the threshold of a thrilling transportation future. Recalling that the automobile was the "supersonic plane of its day," he ventured these forecasts:

> Accidents—"Electronically controlled bumpers may make collisions impossible by applying brakes faster than a human reflex can act."
> Icy Roads—Science may devise means "to heat city streets and highways which will keep them free from ice and snow."
> Parking Problem—Solution will come "either in underground garages, or in tall, thin parking skyscrapers."
> Getting Home in a Hurry—It may be possible "to drive onto a highway, throw a switch, and give the operation of a car completely to electronic control, with the driver riding the beam and with the steering, speed, and braking being done electronically."
> Atomic Energy—"Amazing things can be expected in revolutionizing, by atomic energy, the propulsion of power of cars, trucks and buses."

The American motorist's ability to buy, his facility to use—these factors remain to be determined by tomorrow's conditions. But the forces that make tomorrow already are hard at work. Today's whims and yearnings will continue to provide an economic chain reaction. The system so stimulated is at present employing one out of seven persons in the nation. It also is keeping the motorist busy—busy meeting time payments, paying insurance premiums, attending to his car's upkeep, and planning to replace it, as soon as possible, with a newer model.

Social scientists may debate the wisdom of a civilization so expending its energies. But the fact remains that more persons are participating in this economic cycle than ever before.

What motivates them? Perhaps the fact that Americans aren't content unless they are in motion. Nothing like the automobile yet has come along that so amply fulfills their urge to go "from here to there sitting down."

At a bit past mid-century, it's too early to predict how far advanced is the revolution wrought by the automobile. No doubt it is in an early stage. For as long as space and time remain a challenge to man, the American will be out to conquer them.